I THINK IT'S A SIGN
THAT THE PUN ALSO RISES
DAD JOKES, PUNS, QUIPS, LAUGHS, GROANERS, AND PLAYFUL PENSIVE PONDERINGS

MARK LESLIE

Stark Publishing

Stark Entertainment
An Imprint of Stark Publishing
Waterloo, Ontario
www.starkpublishing.ca

I Think It's A Sign That The Pun Also Rises / Mark Leslie
October 2025

Hardcover ISBN: 978-1-998331-28-4
Paperback ISBN: 978-1-998331-26-0
eBook ISBN: 978-1-998331-27-7

DEDICATION

This one is for my two dads.

*Eugene Lionel Lefebvre, my dad,
and Edward Jean, my birth father.*

*You each had a way with stupid jokes that I
couldn't help but laugh at. Thanks for the
relentless inspiration in manufacturing and
delivering groaners.*

*This one is also for all the folks in the Lexington
neighborhood of Waterloo, Ontario.*

*Thanks for taking the time to read, laugh at, and
comment on my silly chalk-board puns and dad
jokes over the years.*

*Your kind words and gestures continually
inspire me to keep sharing.*

TABLE OF CONTENTS

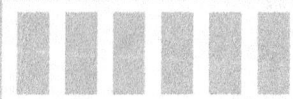

A CHALK BOARD FOR HELPING THE BORED

Introduction

Our house has always been the weird one in our neighborhood. But it wasn't always that way. In fact, it was a relatively normal house until I moved in with my partner, Liz.

When I moved from my apartment in Hamilton and into her Waterloo, Ontario house at the end of 2017 I brought a number of things with me.

Among there were two significant elements from my life: Books and skeletons. I'm of the mind that you can't have too many of either.

For those who are unfamiliar with me and my writing, let me explain a couple of things.

I've been a book nerd my entire life. Books have always played a central role in my life, from the days when I was a child and would eagerly return from my weekly library trip with a pile of books limited by a combination of the check-out cap and how many I could manage to carry to my days as an adult struggling to leave my local bookstore without purchasing another small pile of books to add to my monstrous TBR (to be read) pile.

Okay, so that explains the books. But what about the skeletons?

Well, I've long written darker, spooky, and macabre tales. Many of my short stories (such as the ones collected in my book **One Hand Screaming: 20 Haunting Years**) would be fitting as an episode of *The Twilight Zone* or a darker less tech-focused episode of *Black Mirror*. I've also penned more than half a dozen true ghost story books that include **Haunted Hamilton**, **Spooky Sudbury**, **Creepy Capital**, and **Haunted Hospitals** with **Ghosts of the Great Lakes** coming in 2026.

When I first started doing in-person appearances as an author with the release of my first book in 2004, I brought a few appropriately themed props with me. Some of them were skulls that sat on the table beside my books. As time went on and more books came out, I started appearing at events with a life-sized skeleton. I named him Barnaby Bones.

Having Barnaby sitting with me at book events was useful in a couple of different ways. He would be a draw for the right type of readers. Folks who see a bald man sitting with a skeleton would rush right over to chat with me and check out my books. It was clear to them that my writing was their cup of tea. As for those whose preferences did not include spooky or macabre tales, well the skeleton was a good warning sign for them to avoid making eye-contact with that crazy bald man sitting beside a skeleton.

As the wear and tear on the plastic skeletons (that's right, I don't own real human skeletons—that would be a bit strange, don't you think?) resulted in broken hands, feet, spines, and ribs, I'd keep replacing the "traveling Barnaby" with an upgraded one. But I couldn't get rid of the less-than-perfect skeletons who'd served me so well. So why not hang on to them for Halloween?

That's another thing about our house in Waterloo. With our nearly dozen skeletons and other spooky decor, Liz and I enjoy leveraging them when making our themed Halloween displays.

Over the past several years the themes have included, *Jaws*, *Friday the 13th*, a carnival (which we called *Boney Island*, parodying the *Coney Island* sign with a grinning skeleton face), and *Bonestock* (our parody of Woodstock).

Speaking of parodies, Liz and I have enjoyed producing a few musical ones over the years. In April of 2020, for example, when we were stuck together in isolation in our home, we spent Easter Weekend (a time we'd normally have all our adult children in the house gathered with us), writing, recording, and producing a video. "Stuck in This House Here with You" was a parody of the Steelers Wheel classic "Stuck in the Middle with You." We figured we'd share a laugh during what was a challenging time for so many.

We followed that one up in May 2020 by doing a parody of the old K-Tel television commercials. Our Kay-Tell commercial was a collection of "Isolation Parody

Songs" where we spoofed clips from "Mad World," "Islands in the Stream," "Walkin' After Midnight," and "There's a Kind of Hush."

Liz and I continued to produce videos as the co-hosts for the annual live-streamed Canada's Aurora Awards (run by the Canadian Science Fiction and Fantasy Association, CSFFA) for 2020, 2022, 2023, 2024 and 2025. For each of these, we created a humorous opening schtick inspired by the funny intros that Billy Crystal used to do to open the Academy Awards. And of course, this is because we love to laugh, and to make others laugh.

Which leads us back to the weird house, the skeletons, and the silly jokes that comprise the content of this book.

At one point Liz designed and built a beautiful bench to put in the front yard. I jokingly added one of our skeletons to it one year the day after Halloween with a sign that said "364 days until Halloween!" I kept the count-down going for a while, then added a Santa Claus hat to the skeleton, keeping him out there, as it made people smile (or at least do a double-take) when they were walking or driving by.

Barnaby's outfits changed as the seasons did. We added a St. Patrick's Day hat, bunny ears for Easter, sunglasses in the summer.

When the Covid-19 pandemic took hold in March of 2020, I noticed a lot more people walking through the neighborhood. We were all isolated in our homes, and going for a walk was a way to get some fresh air, exercise, and a different perspective of the world instead of being trapped in one's home.

Considering the stress and anxiety we were all feeling, I wanted to do something to make people smile or even laugh.

I created a sign inspired from a classic Monty Python skit about The Ministry for Silly Walks and a video I'd seen online of how someone in the US had done something similar. I put it in the front yard close to the sidewalk.

It read:

NOTICE

This property is an official jurisdiction of
The Ministry of Silly Walks.
Commence Silly Walking Immediately!

It had a series of silhouettes of John Cleese in various stages of the silly walk he did in that sketch, and small print on the bottom of the sign read: "No FINES for noncompliance, just potential FUN if you give it a try!"

People were having fun with that. My home office window faces the street, and when I'm working at my standing desk, I can clearly see outside. It was great watching folks stop to read the sign and then try it out. It was particularly lovely to see a parent or grandparent out with a kid explaining the sign to them, and doing their own silly walk before encouraging the young person to give it a try.

That was delightful.

But I wanted to do more. Because people really needed a distraction and something to smile or laugh about. And if they'd already seen that sign it wouldn't be as unique or entertaining to them over time.

Sure, I could continue dressing up Barnaby the skeleton in different hats and costumes. Or I could do something that was quicker and easier for me to do: share some of the goofy dad jokes, silly one-liners, and funny written memes I was already sharing on social media.

So, Liz made me a sign board using chalk paint and I started sharing those silly jokes on the sign beside the grinning skeleton. I did my best to change the joke every day.

They were a hit. Folks loved them.

There was a challenge, though. Whenever it rained, the precipitation would wipe clear my funny joke. I crowd-sourced ideas on how to eliminate that via an online community social media site and someone brilliantly suggested that I place the sign above the garage door protected from the rain under the eave of the house.

That worked magnificently. And that is where the sign has remained ever since.

For a while, shortly after putting up a new joke, I started sharing them as short video clips with a #morningcoffeereflections hashtag on TikTok and Instagram. In those videos, I delivered the stupid pun and then took a sip of my coffee as my "mic drop" moment.

But there were far more chalk-written goofy puns and dad jokes on that board outside our house than videos. Partially because going onto social media ended up distracting me from getting actual writing or other important work done.

Sometimes I'd discover a half dozen new jokes, and since I only changed the board daily, I started writing them on scraps of paper so I could remember to use them in the following days. And after a couple of years of putting the jokes up I realized I might be repeating some jokes because I never kept track of which ones I'd already used. So, I adapted to making a note of the jokes I encountered and used on my board into a Google spreadsheet.

Also, over time, Liz insisted that I stopped putting up any jokes that leveraged scatological humor. And, because there's an elementary school just down the street, with plenty of younger people who started to stop to read the signs along with their parents, I also refrained from putting up any of the more adult-themed humor or content.

But I did still track them into my spreadsheet. And yes, considering my passion for not being able to pass up on slipping in a groaner wherever I can, I do often call it my dadda-base of dad jokes.

This book is a collection of the jokes that made it to the "daily chalkboard" along with others that never did and likely never will. In the interest of attribution, wherever I know the source, I include a reference to the comedian or writer who first shared or came up with the one-liner or joke that appears in this book. I also have included several visual meme funnies that I've encountered and shared on social media throughout this book. Some of them have been licensed for use while others are ones that I created or re-created for use here.

In any case, I do hope this book brings you some joy. The world has become so divisive lately. People are filled with endless anxiety and tension. One of the things I love about being a writer is that my stories and novels can help provide an escape from that tension. But in the case of this book, it's about wanting to provide some laughs, a few smiles, and definitely a handful of those eyerolls and groans.

Because, after all, stupid punny jokes are how eye roll.

And maybe some of the funnies contained within this book are ones you're able to add to your own repertoire and share with someone else who could use a laugh. As the saying goes, "laugh and the world laughs with you." And as I believe Bob Newhart continued that classic phrase, "prov and you provolone."

May your day include many smiles, and much laughter.

Mark Leslie
October 2025

META JOKES AND SELF-REFERENCIAL HUMOR

The dadder the better

Jokes that are about dad jokes themselves, include very specific "dad" references within them, or are jokes about jokes.

A priest, a minister, and a rabbi walk into a bar. The bartender looks at them and says, 'What is this, a joke?

—

Why did the dad joke cross the road?
To get to the other sigh.

I had a great library joke to share, but I had to return it.

—

Kid: I'll call you later.
Dad: Please call me dad.

—

I was going to share a joke about trickle-down economics, but 99% of you wouldn't get it.

—

You might think a regular joke becomes a dad joke when it's fully groan. But that's not true, it's when the punchline becomes apparent.

—

The best way to measure a dad joke is with a sighsmoregraph.

—

My dad was trying to make a joke about retirement. It did not work.

—

Dad: What is the difference between a piano, a tuna, and glue?
Kid: I don't know.
Dad: You can tuna piano, but you can't piano a tuna.
Kid: What about the glue?
Dad: I knew you'd get stuck on that.

Every time my dad puts the car in reverse he says: "Ah, this takes me back."

—

I always thought that dad jokes were for groan-ups.

—

> **Kid**: Did you get a haircut?
> **Dad**: No, I got them all cut.

—

I never ran a marathon in 2021. I didn't do one in 2022, 2023, or 2024 either. This is a running joke.

—

Me: Did you know there was a complex named after you?
Oedipus: Well of course. I'm not surprised. I was king. I defeated the sphinx. I stopped a plague. Which part of my extraordinary life is it named after?
Me:
Oedipus: What part of...er, what did they name it after?

—

I had a really happy childhood. My dad used to put me in tires and roll me down hills. Those were Goodyears.

—

I save all my dad jokes in my dadda-base.

Here's a joke for all you mind readers out there:

—

Stephen King has a song named Joe. I'm not Joe King. But he is.

—

The day my son was born I bumped into another dad at the nursery who congratulated me, saying his daughter was born the day before. He smiled and said, "Maybe when they're older they'll meet, fall in love, and get married." I smiled back but didn't respond. As if my son would marry someone twice his age.

—

What do you get when you cross a joke with a rhetorical question?

—

I once submitted 10 jokes into a contest, thinking with that many submissions, one was sure to be a winner. Sadly, no pun in ten did.

—

I've noticed that they've started to put jokes on the back of bacon packages now. Get this one I recently spotted. It reads: "One serving = 2 slices."

I was going to tell you a joke about time travel, but you didn't like it.

—

I wanted to make a dad joke about sodium...but NA.

—

Poop jokes aren't my favorite type of joke, but they're a solid #2.

—

Science puns make me numb. But math jokes make me number.

—

I like telling dad jokes. And sometimes he laughs.

—

The problem with political jokes is sometimes they get elected.

—

The other day I met Bruce Lee's vegetarian brother, Brocco Lee. And his other brother who can't take a joke, Serious Lee. And the one who does everything at the last minute, Sudden Lee.

—

I was going to share a joke about a piece of paper, but I thought better of it, because it's tearable.

I could share a joke about pizza, but it's a little cheesy.

—

I was going to tell you a joke about construction, but I'm still working on it.

—

I was going to tell you a joke about time travel, but you didn't like it.

—

I was going to tell you a space pun, but I need more time to planet.

—

If you tell a joke in the forest, but nobody laughs, was it still a joke? (Attribution: *Stephen Wright*)

—

Those who like my jokes are happier, more intelligent, and better looking according to a survey I just made up.

—

I was on the train to work, and the conductor told me he had to charge me extra for telling dad jokes. I said. "That's not fare!"

—

My son told me he wants to be a skydiver when he grows up. I told him that was a descent career choice.

Want to hear a joke about a roof? The first one is on the house.

—

My dad was in his early 60's when he was driving to work, and a wheel fell off his car. That was the day he thought it was a good idea to retire.

—

The difference between a bad joke and a dad joke is one letter.

—

If you tell dad jokes but you don't have kids, you might be a Faux Pa.

—

I tried to write a joke about infinity. But it didn't have an ending.

—

Elevator jokes are so good because they work on many levels.

—

I told a chemistry joke once. There was no re-action.

—

Once upon a time, a joke tried to tell itself. It got stuck in an infinite time loop and never delivered.

PEOPLE WHO LAUGH AT DAD'S JOKES

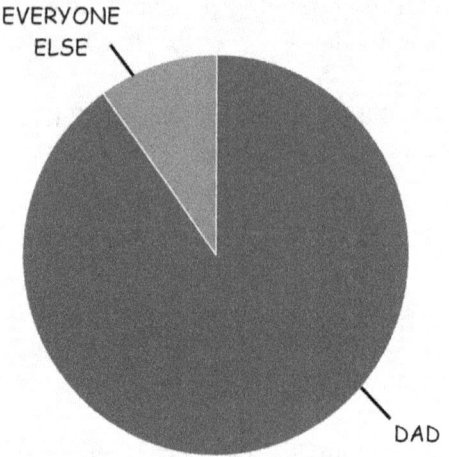

EVERYONE ELSE

DAD

DAD JOKES, BAD JOKES, PUNS, AND ONE-LINERS

A random selection of silliness

BAD PUNS ARE HOW EYE ROLL

Groan, laugh, or smile as you read through this collection of zaniness.

My wife asked me to put ketchup on the shopping list. Now I can't read it.

—

Did you hear about the adjacent houses that fell in love? It was one of those lawn-distance relationships.

—

It was a sad and disappointing day when I discovered my universal remote did not, in fact, control the Universe. Not even remotely.

If you're ringing in the New Year, you might just have tinnitus.

—

I entered the World Kleptomaniac Championship Tournament. I took gold, silver, and bronze.

—

I changed my iPhone name to "Titanic." It's finally syncing.

—

Sixty-three earths can fit inside Uranus. One day I'll be mature enough to read this fact without laughing.

—

Last night as I was walking home, I passed a lemon loaf pie, a mayonnaise cheesecake, and a cold fudge sundae. I remember thinking: "The streets are strangely desserted tonight."

—

My fear of moving stairs is escalating.

—

I have a friend in the UK who calls elevators a lift. I guess we were raised differently.

—

New Year's Resolutions are more of a "to do" list that you attend to the first week of January and then promptly lose.

I wonder if Leprechauns are just Santa's Elves who got fired for drinking on the job.

—

If you're watching a parade, make sure you stand in one spot. Don't follow it. It never changes. And if the parade is boring, run in the opposite direction. You will fast forward the parade. (Attribution: *Mitch Hedberg*)

—

A once worked at a factory that made ok products. It was a satisfactory job.

—

I accidentally got some deodorant spray in my mouth this morning. So I'm now speaking with a slight Axe scent.

—

I struggle with Roman numerals until I get to 159. Then it just CLIX.

—

A friend of mine was recently fired from a company. As they walked him out, they handed him a bag of coffee saying it was grounds for termination.

—

Never make snow angels in a dog park.

—

Do race horses slow down when they see police horses?

A poker player friend of mine who recently broke his arm is having a hard time dealing with it.

—

I have set two goals:
  1) To get myself back into the shape I was before the accident.
  2) To stop referring to my years of overeating as "the accident."

—

I was going to write a book about spaghetti, but I couldn't get pasta first line.

—

My doctor prescribed me a new cream that's supposed to stop me from gloating so much. I can't wait to rub it in.

—

Some people these days are just far too judgmental. I can tell just by looking at them.

—

My spouse left me due to my gambling addiction. But I'm pretty sure I can win her back.

—

The other day my niece delivered a beautiful baby boy. I just knew she had it in her.

—

Cat puns really freak meowt. I'm not kitten.

Some people have trouble sleeping, but I can do it with my eyes closed.

—

It was so cold the other day that my computer froze. But it was my own fault for leaving so many Windows open.

—

I'm no longer allowed to go caroling at the local psychiatric hospital. I guess "Do You Hear What I Hear?" was a bad choice?

—

If at first you don't succeed, then skydiving isn't for you.

—

Someone recently broke into our house and stole the medals I won from a series of limbo tournaments. How low can you go?

—

I was addicted to the hokey pokey. But I turned myself around.

—

People are usually shocked when they find out I'm not a good electrician.

—

If Genghis Khan, so kahn you.

—

My poor knowledge of Greek Mythology has always been my Achilles elbow.

Your nose is in the middle of your face because it is the scenter.

—

You'd be advised not to fart in an Apple store because they don't have Windows.

—

The umbrella was originally supposed to be called "the brella." But the inventor hesitated.

—

I'm going to start a support group for procrastinators. Tomorrow.

—

When I was younger, I couldn't decide between being a psychiatrist or a writer. So I flipped a coin: Heads or Tales.

—

It is a fifteen-minute walk from my house to the closest bar. It's a forty-five-minute walk back home. The difference is staggering.

—

A friend of mine who is a monk recently saw the face of Jesus imprinted in a tub of margarine. He said, "I can't believe it's not Buddha!"

—

When I die, bury me with my entire record collection. It'll be my vinyl resting place.

It's a shame about that massive explosion at the cheese factory in France. All that was left was de Brie.

—

Someone threw a bottle of Omega-3 pills at my head. It hurt, but my injuries were only super fish oil.

—

I'm not sure what the best thing about living in Switzerland is, but the flag is a big plus.

—

I've recently taken up Silent Tennis. It's like regular tennis, but without the racquet.

—

E was the only letter of the alphabet that got something from Santa, because all the other letters were not E.

—

My LEGO® set said right on the box: 7 to 10 years. But I finished it in under 3 hours.

—

I have a friend named Gemma Pell. She has a heck of time whenever she tries to introduce herself in French.

—

If you get into a pillow fight with Death, you should be prepared for the reaper cushions.

You know what actually makes me smile? My facial muscles.

—

It was sad to read about the inventor of autocorrect recently dying. The funnel is going to be held tomato.

—

Want to know how to keep a person in suspense? I'll tell you tomorrow.

—

They say that the early bird gets the worm. If that's the case, I'm sleeping in. Maybe they serve pancakes and bacon later in the morning.

—

If attractive people are considered "eye candy" then I'm probably somewhere in the "liver and onions" group.

—

I've started to keep my guitar in the car with me whenever I drive. It comes in handy during traffic jams.

—

I once dated a woman who was an avid magazine collector. She had issues.

—

I like puns about eyes. The cornea the better.

The correct way to spell hats is HATS; because it's all caps.

—

I'm really not sure why pirates are called pirates. I just know they arrr!

—

The other day I was mugged by six dwarves. Not Happy.

—

I'm writing a book on how to fall down a flight of stairs. It's a step-by-step guide.

—

A friend of mine who is a sound technician in a theatre got really drunk the other day. He had one two one two one two many.

—

I was once arrested for drinking battery acid. But I wasn't charged.

—

Santa doesn't have to pay to park his sleigh because it's on the house.

—

I hate to brag, but the other day I finished a jigsaw puzzle in just a matter of hours. And on the box, it said 2 to 4 years.

—

When it comes to having a party in space you have to planet.

I once sued an airline for losing my luggage. I lost my case.

—

Some pirates can never finish the alphabet, because they get lost at C.

—

A vegan might say that people who sell meat are disgusting, but people who sell fruit and vegetables are grocer.

—

Penguins produce an oil that coats their feathers and helps them retain heat. So it's true what they say: The oily bird gets the warm.

—

The waiter warned me when setting the plate on my table that it was really hot. I assured him I would be okay as I wasn't really attracted to plates.

—

If you can't master the guitar, don't fret.

—

Stop all that hating on people who are being too lazy. They didn't even do anything.

—

I heard that Spider-Man has a winter coat made out of Mediterranean flat bread. It's a Pita Parka.

The only day of the year that orders you to do something is March 4th.

—

People keep saying "It is what it is." But seriously, what is it?

—

Alligators can live for up to 100 years, which is why there's a pretty good reason you'll see them later.

—

I may not have lost all of my marbles just yet. But there's definitely a small hole in the bag somewhere.

—

I received a flyer on anger management the other day. But I lost it.

—

A storm blew away 25% of our roof last night. Oof.

—

I was upset and complained to my carpenter that I'd explained before he started the job that I wanted carpeting on my steps. He gave me a blank stare.

—

I bought a pair of shoes with memory foam insoles. No more forgetting what I walked into the kitchen for.

I think it's okay to lie to your dentist, because sometimes the tooth hurts.

—

People often mistake me for an adult because of my age.

—

I just turned wine into vomit. Your move, Jesus

—

I hate Daylight Savings time so much I lost sleep over it.

—

I am reading this amazing book about a 4.4-pound bird. It's called: "Two Kilo Mockingbird."

—

The spelling of Irish names is my pet piamh.

—

Lance may be an uncommon name these days, but in Medieval times, people were named Lance a lot.

—

I recently converted our attic into a workspace for a new boat-building business. Sails are going through the roof.

—

When my friend Joyce learned how to clone herself, she rejoiced.

Today when I went to the grocery store, I had the slowest, nastiest, and meanest cashier ever. That's the last time I'll be using the self-checkout line.

—

I'm working on a new television documentary about how to fly a plane. Right now, we're filming the pilot.

—

The person who invented the Ferris Wheel never met the person who invented the Merry Go Round. I suppose it's because they traveled in different circles.

—

The only thing Flat-Earthers have to fear is sphere itself.

—

They say that the average person will eat about 25 spiders in their lifetime. But really, you can eat as many as you wish. Treat yourself. You deserve it.

—

Did you know that almost all garden gnomes have tiny red hats? It's a little gnome fact.

—

My friend accidentally drank some invisible ink. He's now at the hospital waiting to be seen.

I have started investing in stocks. Beef, chicken, and vegetable. One day I hope to be a bouillonaire.

—

I hate it when people accuse me of lolly gagging when I'm quite clearly dilly dallying.

—

Amal and Juan are identical twins. Their mom only carries one photo of them in her wallet. Because if you've seen Juan, you've seen Amal

—

Astronomers got tired watching the moon go around the earth for 24 hours. So they decided to call it a day.

—

One of the most amazing and historic displays of democracy, is that a thousand islands managed to come together and agree on a single dressing.

—

To all the people who said I'd never amount to anything because of my procrastination, just you wait!

—

I poured root beer into a square glass, and now I have a glass of beer.

A Buddist monk walks up to a hot dog stand and says: "Make me one with everything." He hands the vendor a twenty, expecting change. But the vendor shrugs and says: "Change comes from within."

—

Green is my favorite color. I love it even more than blue and yellow combined.

—

I know a writer who broke up with their pencil because it was too sketchy.

—

My boss said I intimidate my coworkers. I started at him until he apologized.

—

If you let then Shenan once, they'll Shenanigan.

—

God grant me the confidence and perseverance of a typo that's survived through 45 rounds of edits.

—

I know a guy who is addicted to brake fluid. He says he can stop anytime he wants.

—

I recently spotted a Vietnamese Italian fusion restaurant called Pho-gettaboutit

I once suffered from an addiction to seaweed. I needed to sea kelp.

—

To whomever stole my copy of Microsoft Office, I will find you. You have my Word!

—

Years ago, I had to part ways with a friend who just wouldn't stop counting. I wonder what he's up to now.

—

I used to hate facial hair. But then it grew on me.

—

I sometimes wonder what my parents did to fight boredom before the internet. I asked my eighteen brothers and sisters, and they didn't know either.

—

My friend bought me a telekinetic abacus for my birthday! It wasn't my favorite present, but it's the thought that counts!

—

My friend David had his ID stolen. We just call him Dav now.

—

If you suck at playing a brass instrument, that's probably why.

Some anonymous person keeps sending me celery. It feels like I'm being stalked.

—

"Do what you love, and the money will follow," they say. So, I ate a pizza, drank some beer, and read a book. Now, I wait.

—

If Mediums can communicate with the dead, just imagine what a Large can do.

—

Claustrophobia is a fear of closed spaces. For example, I'm going to the beer store later today and I'm scared it might be closed before I arrive.

—

I called my landlord to say I had a leak in my sink. He said: "That's fine. I'm not judging."

—

Bros don't let other bros walk around with open flies. It's called our zip code.

—

Justice is a dish best served cold. If it were served warm it would be justwater.

—

Word of advice: Do not drink while wrapping Christmas presents. BTW, if anyone gets a gift television remote control from me this year, I'm going to need it back.

I got kicked out of the coffee club because I wore a tea shirt.

—

I've misplaced Dwayne Johnson's cutting instrument for his origami workshop. I can't believe I've lost the Rock's paper scissors.

—

I saw a snake that was 3.14 meters long. I think it was a πthon.

—

One tectonic plate bumped into another and said: "Sorry, my fault!"

—

I hope Elon Musk never gets into a scandal because ElonGate would be really drawn out.

—

One of the things I just can't deal with is a deck of cards glued together.

—

Is it crazy how saying sentences backwards creates backwards sentences saying how crazy it is?

—

My wife threatened to divorce me if a gave our daughter a silly name. So I called her Bluff.

I've done some really terrible things for money. Like getting up early to go to work.

—

The first rule of "Condescending Club" is rather complex, and I don't think you'd understand it even if I explained it in the simplest terms.

—

One hundred years ago many people owned a horse and only the rich had cars. Today, many people own a car and only the rich have horses. My how the stables have turned.

—

My landlord wants to talk to me about the high heating bill. I told him my door is always open.

—

If the USA is so great, then why did someone create the USB?

—

Fruit farmers eat what they can and can what they can't

—

I'm taking steps to overcome my wilderness hiking addiction. I'm not out of the woods yet.

Great hide and seek players are really hard to find.

—

Laughing out loud in Hawaii is forbidden, because it's a low ha state

—

When you dream in color it's a pigment of your imagination.

—

Boarding school taught me how to get on an airplane.

—

Went on a date and everything was going great until she asked: "Boxers or briefs?" I said, "Depends." And then she left.

—

The other day I saw a police officer dressed in a flight attendant uniform. I was confused until I realized it was a cop in plane clothing.

—

Inspecting mirrors is a job I could really see myself doing.

—

Every night for the past week I keep waking from this horrible recurring dream where, whenever I step outside the house, I'm run over by a bike. It's a vicious cycle.

To make a long story short I became an editor.

—

I went to the paint store to get thinner. It didn't work. So I joined a gym.

—

When the dentist married the manicurist, they fought tooth and nail.

—

I made a chicken salad last night but apparently, they prefer grain.

—

My partner and I laugh at how competitive we both are about everything. But I laugh more.

—

My therapist said I have trouble expressing emotions. I can't say I'm surprised.

—

The other day I watched a documentary on how beavers construct their homes. It was the best dam documentary I've ever seen.

—

My online banking passwords was hacked... again. That's the fifth time I've had to change the name of our dog.

Mountains aren't funny. They are hill areas.

I have a boomerang that won't come back. I call it a stick.

—

Everyone who signed my Grade 7 yearbook will be happy to learn that I did, in fact "Stay Cool!"

—

If a tree is cut down in the forest and it understands why, is it still stumped?

—

There's a new dating app for bald people that's completely free. That's right, you don't have toupee.

—

Ants never get sick because they have little anty bodies.

—

To spell the word "Panda" you just need a P AND A.

—

My wife called and told me she spotted a fox on her way to work. I asked her how she knew it was on its way to work. She hung up on me.

—

I just found out that "Aaaarrrrrggghhh" isn't a real world. I can't even tell you how angry I am.

The adjective for metal is metallic. But it's not so for iron...which is ironic.

—

I'm reading a book about a couple of insects who fall in love in an Italian city. It's a Rome ants novel.

—

I never realized that cottage cheese isn't cheese at all. It's just a curd to me.

—

I was outnumbered when 1, 3, 5, 7, and 9 attacked me! And yes, the odds were against me!

—

People write "congrats" because they can't spell "congrajalashins."

—

A rare worn-down pencil belonging to William Shakespeare has been discovered. Experts are not sure if the pencil is 2B or not 2B.

—

A friend of mine made a belt entirely out of old watches. I think it's a waist of time.

—

If I had a dollar for every time I was suspicious, I'd wonder who was paying me and why.

I recently took a pole and found that 100% of the people in the tent did NOT like it.

—

Someone threw a full jar of mayonnaise at me. I turned and said: "What the Hellman?"

—

Did you hear about the two guys who stole a calendar? They each got six months.

—

Before the crowbar was invented crows had to drink at home.

—

Someone called my puns childish. But we all know that they're fully groan.

—

I recently did some successful funding for a carnival. You could say I raised a fair amount.

—

I'm a trophy husband. More of a participation trophy though.

—

I lost my application for building a house on a piece of land I purchased. I'm not going to dwell on it.

—

My dog Minton chewed up my racket and my shuttlecock. Bad Minton!

Tips on how to fall asleep in a chair.
  1) Be old.
  2) Sit in a chair.

—

A have a friend who is a social vegan. He avoids meet.

—

I went to the store to pick up 8 cans of Sprite. But when I got home, I realized I only picked 7 up.

—

Optimist: The glass is 1/2 full
Pessimist: The glass is 1/2 empty
Excel: The glass is January 2

—

I never finish anything. I have a black belt in partial arts.

—

I often sing when I'm driving my car. But my friend only joins in when we're going in reverse. He's my backup singer.

—

I told my friends I'd stop making furniture puns. Sofa, so good.

—

I heard that a group of scientists invented the world's largest suction cup. I have no idea how they pulled that off.

To drive an electric car, you must possess a current driver's license.

—

I introduced my friend to minimalism. It was the least I could do.

—

"I'm fine," is the most common lie told. "I have read and agree to the terms and conditions," is the second most common lie told.

—

I Googled "missing medieval servant." It returned with: "page not found.

—

I've never understood why you'd pay to have pizza delivered when you could just order it without liver in the first place.

—

I'm running the Scandinavian marathon. It starts in Norway and ends at the Finnish line.

—

The one letter that can keep pirates straight is "p." Without it, they are irate.

—

"I need help with this crossword!" my girlfriend yelled, almost in tears. "It's 9 letters, another word for 'concentration.'" I think she's seeking attention.

Meteorologists have weighed rainbows and found out they're pretty light.

—

Before Sigourney Weaver, people had to weave their sigournies by hand.

—

I read a book called "The Ten Best Ways To Clean Your Pig." It was complete hogwash.

—

My dog is pretty smart. Yesterday I asked him: "What's 2 minus 2." He said nothing.

—

When driving you should keep your eyes on the road and your head out of your apps.

—

I'll take the high road. You take the psycho path.

—

Obtuse angles are often depressed because they're never right.

—

If you ever get locked out of your house, talk to the door lock calmly. Communication is the key.

—

One major difference between men and women is that if a woman says "Smell this," it usually smells nice.

I'm going to start collecting highlighters. Mark my words!

—

My child has decided to start studying burrowing animals. I said, "Gopher it."

—

Radioactive cats have 18 half-lives.

—

Without freedom of speech, we would not know who the idiots are.

—

I think we should have mind-controlled air fresheners. It makes scents when you think about it.

—

When algebra teachers retire how do they deal with the aftermath?

—

Water is heavier than butane because butane is a lighter fluid.

—

If you like the farmer's daughter you might do something to a tractor.

—

My friend Jack converses with all the plants that grown in his garden. And the legumes speak back to him. That's right, Jack and the beans talk.

This morning when I was taking a walk I was hit by a violin, a clarinet, and then a French horn. I think it was an orchestrated attack!

—

My view on toilet paper rolls is over the top.

—

I'm pining for a good tree pun. I wish they were more poplar.

—

A new LEGO® store had their grand opening downtown the other day. People were lined up for blocks.

—

I pulled a muscle while digging for gold. It's just a miner injury.

—

Did you hear about the fired stage designer who left town without making a scene?

—

My friend who is a cosmology student missed class and was forced to take a makeup test.

—

If you have to wear a mask when you already wear glasses, you may be entitled to condensation.

—

Sea monsters eat fish and ships.

I wanted to be a monk, but I never got the chants.

—

I once drank a milkshake while standing on the edge of a cliff. It was ledge and dairy.

—

You make antifreeze by stealing her blankets.

—

I was told never to steal kitchen utensils. But it's a whisk I'm willing to take.

—

Photons don't check bags at the airport because they are traveling light.

—

I was watching a spring fly fishing tournament. It was broadcast on live stream.

—

We named our dog Rolex. He's our watchdog.

—

If your eyes hurt from excessive screen time, there's a nap for that.

—

Out of all my body parts, my eyeballs are in the best shape, because I roll them something like 300 times a day.

—

When the fog lifts in Hollywood, UCLA.

My relationship with whiskey is on the rocks.

—

Years ago, I dated a tennis player. But sadly, love meant nothing to her.

—

They say a banana is good for cleaning your colon. It was much later, I realized they were talking about eating them.

—

I want to make pancakes for breakfast but I keep waffling.

—

A male staff member at a downtown night club fell off the roof the other night. All authorities have confirmed for sure is he was not a bouncer.

—

I recently found a recipe for leftover bacon. I've never heard of that kind of bacon. Is it new?

—

I have a fear of over-engineered buildings. It's a complex complex complex.

—

I love board games. My favorite is when people put meat, cheese, some fruit and crackers on a board. I'm so good at that one.

Resolutions are in one year and out the other.

—

I saw a baguette at the zoo. It was bread in captivity.

—

I got a new job as a guillotine operator. Beheading there shortly.

—

I always wear glasses when I do math. It improves division.

—

Today I learned that "Wet Floors" is not a request.

—

I surprised my wife with a new fridge. Her face lit up when she opened it.

—

In Anthens, it's rare for people to wake before noon because Dawn is tough on Greece.

—

The difference between Iron Man & Aluminum Man is Iron man stops the bad guys, Aluminum Man just foils them.

—

I believe pencils are superior to pens, especially for filling out crossword puzzles. Does that make me erasist?

I looked up the word opaque. The definition wasn't clear.

—

Someone asked me what the 9th letter of the alphabet was. It was a complete guess, but I was right.

—

My father got a new stair lift. It's driving him up the wall.

—

No matter how good the hand soap smells, never walk out of the bathroom sniffing your fingers.

—

The four seasons of the year are all different. Summer warmer than others.

—

I once dated a girl who was a twin. People often asked me how I could tell them apart. It was easy. Alison painted her nails red. And Bob had a beard.

—

My friend was trying to explain electricity to me, and I was like Watt?

—

People are always amazed at the skilled tattoo artists in Spain. No one expects the Spanish ink precision.

I tried to buy bread at the East Indian grocery store. They had naan.

—

Once I was kidnapped by a pack of mimes. They did unspeakable things to me.

—

The other day I bought a thesaurus, but when I got home and opened it, all the pages were blank. I have no words to describe how angry I am.

—

I call my horse mayo. And sometimes mayo neighs.

—

I was looking for a tuxedo at a fancy man's shop when the store clerk kept hovering so close to me. I asked him to leave me alone. He said, "Fine, suit yourself."

—

The Little Mermaid wears an algebra to math class.

—

I'm waiting for the release of the new movie "Constipated." It hasn't come out yet.

—

I'm eating more donuts. It's the original hole food.

The other night I was attacked by a bunch of circus performers in a parking lot. I won though, cause I went right for the juggler.

—

I never trust trains. They have loco motives.

—

Norwegian war ships have bar codes, so when they arrive at a port you can scan da navy in.

—

There was a huge fight at the local seafood restaurant. There were battered fish everywhere.

—

When baking dog biscuits be sure to use Collie flour.

—

There's a fine line between a numerator and a denominator. And I bet only a fraction of people will find this funny.

—

9 out of 10 dentists refuse to work on a Grizzly unless it has been given a strong sedative. There's safety in numb bears.

I always thought the best way to make holy water was to boil the hell out of it.

It was a terrible summer for Humpty Dumpty. But he had a great fall.

—

A slice of apple pie is $2.50 in Jamaica and $3.00 in the Bahamas. These are the pie rates of the Caribbean.

—

After dinner my wife asked if I could clear the table. I needed a running start, but I made it.

—

A bulldozer is someone who sleeps through political speeches.

—

Did you hear about the comedian who stopped at a fabric store on the way to work? He needed new material.

—

Forklift drivers hate my puns. They find them unpalletable.

—

I've decided that, starting January 1st, I'll only be watching videos in 1080p or higher. It's my New Years Resolution.

Of all my body parts, my fingers are the most reliable. I can always count on them.

Don't let anyone call you average. That's just mean.

—

My wife kicked me out because I refused to stop doing terrible Arnold Schwarzenegger impersonations. But don't worry. I'll return.

—

Kitchen remodelers are counter productive.

—

Your debt will stay with you if you can't budge it.

—

I'm doing a crossword, and I'm stuck on seven down. It's three letters long and the clue is "Lemonade style drink, not Sprite." Oh wait, I'm sorry, that's not seven down. It's 7UP.

—

Australia's biggest export is boomerangs. It's also their biggest import.

—

Wouldn't it be interesting if the really big concerts had a little mini football game in the middle of them?

People talk about the eye of the tiger but rarely discuss any of the other letters.

For chemists alcohol is not a problem. It's a solution.

—

If you think swimming with dolphins is expensive, you should try swimming with sharks. It cost my friend an arm and a leg.

I'm friends with 25 letters of the alphabet. I don't know why.

—

Outdoor Tip: Carry binoculars when hiking so that when you make frequent stops. It looks like you're appreciating nature—not gasping for air and clinging to dear life.

—

Dogs can't operate MRI machines. But catscan.

—

Crushing pop cans is soda pressing.

—

I was going to tell a joke about all of the recent layoffs, but sadly none of them work.

—

Silence is golden. Duct tape is silver.

A buddy of mine got fired from his job at the calendar factory just for taking a day off.

I once had a frog that could jump higher than a house. It was easy, of course. Because houses can't jump.

—

He who laughs last didn't get it.

—

Bad rainbows are sent to prism where they have to reflect on what they've done.

—

I tried to grab the fog. I mist.

—

Five ants rented an apartment with another five ants. Now they're tenants.

—

Cows have hooves because they lactose.

—

I'm proud to say that our house doesn't have any unhealthy snacks in it. Because I ate them all.

—

Apparently "naked hiking" means no GPS, no music, no maps, no distractions. I probably should have looked that up before trying it.

—

I did some financial planning, and it looks like I can retire at 97 and live comfortably for perhaps half an hour.

If you have any bowling puns, please spare me.

—

Remember, if the world didn't suck, we'd all fall off.

—

I swallowed a bunch of synonyms yesterday. It gave me thesaurus throat I've ever had.

—

Turning vegan would be a big missed steak.

—

I've heard that a lot of people pick their nose. Me, I feel as if I was just born with mine.

—

Did you hear about Schrodinger's frog? When the veterinarian told him it had croaked, Schrodinger didn't know if it was alive or dead?

—

Procrastination is a dish best served eventually.

—

I wanted to go on a diet. But I feel like I have too much on my plate right now.

—

I don't mean to brag but the cashiers at our local grocery store keep checking me out.

I'm terrified of elevators. I'm taking steps to avoid them.

—

I've heard that "icy" is one of the easiest words to spell. Looking at it now, I see why.

—

Hippies like exit signs because they're "way out" man.

—

Nothing starts with an N and ends with a G. It's true.

—

I do all my own stunts, but rarely ever intentionally.

—

The difference between a poorly dressed man on a tricycle and a well-dressed man on a bicycle is attire.

—

Puns about communism aren't funny unless everyone gets them.

—

You know it's cold outside when you go outside and it's cold.

—

Although my wife's young, she might be getting dementia, because she keeps saying she doesn't remember what she saw in me.

My friends told me to get help for my drinking, so I hired a bartender.

—

Beer cures what ales ya.

—

No matter how far you push the envelope it remains stationery.

—

Not to brag, but I'm on hold and my call is important to them.

—

I hired a handman and gave him a list of 8 things to do. At the end of the day, he only completed items 1, 3, 5 and 7. It turns out he only does odd jobs.

—

Getting mythology wrong is my Hercules ankle.

—

I hate it when I gain 20 pounds for a role and then remember that I'm not an actor.

—

A lot of women say their husbands never listen to them. I'm proud to say that I've never heard my wife say that.

—

I have a Polish friend who is a sound guy. I have a Czech one too. A Czech one too.

A teacher told me once not to worry about learning correct spelling because in the future there would be spellcheck. For that I am eternally grapefruit.

—

The other day I couldn't figure out if someone was waving at me or someone behind me. In other news, I recently lost my job as a lifeguard.

—

One time for a first date, I suggested that we meet at the gym. She never showed up. That's when I realized we weren't going to work out.

—

I tried reading the dictionary in bed the other night. Didn't finish it. Got up to P.

—

There exists a quantity of artificial butter flavor beyond which people begin to believe it's not butter. This is known as the margarine of error.

—

Last night I had a dream that I was a muffler. I woke up exhausted!

—

We got an electric blanket, so now I call all the other ones acoustic blankets.

I saw a snowman at the farmer's market the other day browsing at the carrot stand. He was picking his nose.

—

In University I studied English Lit. If I'd studied English sober it might have taken me four years instead of six.

—

Do you ever wonder if songbirds get mad at hummingbirds for not knowing the words?

—

My wife is furious about the neighbor who sunbathes naked in her back yard all afternoon. Personally, I'm on the fence.

—

Whenever I'm commuting to work with a bunch of fellow employees and we go through an underpass I get nervous. It must be my carpool tunnel syndrome.

—

An opinion without 3.14 is just an onion.

—

I've always thought that a good term for mansplaining might be "correctile dysfunction."

—

Over 200 years ago two brothers announced they could fly. Turns out they were Wright.

I recently released my own fragrance. Nobody in the car seemed to like it.

—

Volkswagen should bring back the Beetle as an electric car and call it the Lightning Bug.

—

Everybody told Sam not to sing. But regardless, Samsung.

—

Every morning in the shower I play a game where I try to figure out what I bumped into yesterday. I call it "bruise clues."

—

A nervous judge went to the dentist for an extraction and said: "Do you swear to pull the tooth, the whole tooth, and nothing but the tooth?"

—

My friend's partner suddenly left him because of his obsession with astrology. I think he should have seen the signs.

—

My wife is really mad because I have no sense of direction. So I packed up my stuff and right.

—

Melons have weddings because they cantaloupe.

Of all the inventions in the past 100 years the dry erase board is the most remarkable.

—

I invented a new word today: plagiarism!

—

Singing in the shower is fun until you get soap in your mouth. Then it becomes a soap opera.

—

My new girlfriend used to date a circus clown. Not sure how I feel about that, other than, those are some pretty big shoes to fill.

—

Alaskan eye doctors are optical Aleutians.

—

Sometimes before bed I fall asleep on my couch. It's a little sleep appetizer. A nappieizer.

—

It takes guts to be an organ donor.

—

You know how teams sometimes throw the ball into the crowd after they win the game? That's not allowed in bowling. I know that now.

—

Bruce Lee was fast. His brother Sudden Lee, was faster.

Eyelashes are supposed to prevent things from getting into your eyes. But whenever I have something in my eye it's usually an eyelash. Now that's eyeronic.

—

I used to work in a shoe-recycling shop. It was sole destroying.

—

For the longest time I've only wanted to play pool so long as I get the first shot. It's a habit that I need to break.

—

My wife told me I had to stop acting like a flamingo. So I had to put my foot down.

—

I hate when someone uses the wrong word and doesn't have the humidity to admit it.

—

I like saying the word "drool." It just rolls off the tongue.

—

Learning French has really encouraged me to live in the moment, particularly because I can't yet conjugate any other verb tense.

—

I once knew a guy named Hunter who was vegan. We nicknamed him Gatherer because we thought that would be hilarious.

What did the pirate say on his 80th birthday? Aye Matey!

—

Taller people sleep longer in beds.

—

Librarians tell me that checking out books is good for your circulation.

—

I'm going to stand outside. So, if anyone asks, I'm outstanding.

—

Last night I accidentally glued my finger and thumb together. I'll be okay for a while.

—

Someone ripped the fifth month out of my calendar. I'm dis-Mayed.

—

My buddy who is a film maker says he accidentally shot 12 minutes of his feet instead of the actor who was performing the scene. He says it's still some great footage.

—

The first rule of Dunning-Kruger club is you don't know you're in Dunning-Kruger club.

—

How many storm troopers does it take to change a lightbulb? None, because they are all on the dark side.

Carpe diem = seize the day.
Imodium = don't sneeze today.

—

I once ate a frozen apple. It was hard core.

—

I lost my job as a bank teller when this lady asked me to check her balance, and I pushed her over.

—

I got an A on my origami assignment when I turned my paper into my teacher.

—

We have two unwritten rules in this house:
1.
2.

—

Scientists recorded two helium atoms laughing. HeHe.

—

My friend Cliff is always telling me to drop over sometime.

—

Have you ever heard about the kidnapping at school? It's okay, he woke up.

I just bought one of the best presents for my buddy's kid's birthday. Broken drums! You can't beat them.

I found a book called How to Solve 50% of Your Problems. So I bought 2.

—

Not to brag, but they hired me as a fitness model. They used me as the "before" model.

—

What does a nosey pepper do? It gets jalapeño business.

—

Did you ever wake up, kiss the person sleeping beside you, and feel glad that you're alive? I just did, and apparently, I'm no longer welcome to fly Air Canada.

—

I stayed up all night wondering where the sun went. Then it dawned on me.

—

I learned how to make Budweiser. You teach him to read.

—

I heard that a local lifeguard was unable to save a drowning hippie because he was too far out, man.

—

If a bee is bothering you don't swat at it or run away. Just stare at it. Because seeing is bee leaving.

I overheard a mother broom tell her baby broom that it was time to go to sweep.

—

I think that of all the days, Saturday and Sunday are the strongest. The rest are weekdays.

—

I'd like to offer a shout out to all the sidewalks out there for keeping me off the streets.

—

I'm reading a horror story in braille. Something bad is going to happen, I can just feel it.

—

I thought I would write a new drinking song. But I got a bit confused after the first few bars.

—

My Teddy Bear turned down a slice of delicious cake because he was stuffed.

—

I was raised as an only child. It drove my sister nuts.

—

My wife left a note on the refrigerator door saying "This isn't working. Goodbye." I opened the fridge, and it's working just fine.

I think I know how to make 7 even. Take away the S.

—

I'm getting totally fed up with people complaining about rising prices. $2.50 for iced tea. $3.00 for coffee. $4.00 for a slice of cake. $5.00 to park the car. Any more complaining and I'm going to stop inviting people over.

—

I found this great place to order sausage online. I'll send you a link.

—

We have two dogs. They're named Calvin and Klein. That's right, they're a pair of boxers.

—

I just found out that there was a neighborhood meeting about the weirdo who lives on our block. Strange that they didn't invite me.

—

Why is it spelled "camouflage" and not   ?

—

My buddy was dating a social media manager who recently broke up with him. I heard it was because of the lack of engagement.

The guy who stole my diary went missing. My thoughts are with his family.

—

Don't accept a friend request from Dan Druff. He is really flaky and won't stay out of your hair.

—

I was thinking of trying that new all-almond diet. But that's just nuts.

—

I knew this woman who broke up with a friend of mine because he only had 5 of his toes. He lost the one which he lost from his left foot in a lawn mower accident when he was younger. After she broke it off, my friend said he had no idea she was lack toes intolerant.

—

I'd like to thank whoever told my mom that WFT means "wow that's fantastic." Her texts are much more fun now.

—

I sleep better naked. Why can't the flight attendants understand this?

—

One of them main differences between me and Superman is he has super vision while I require supervision.

I can tell if someone is lying just by looking at them. I can also tell if they're standing up.

—

Someone recently accused me of plagiarism. Their words, not mine.

—

I had a beer the other night and on the side of the can it read "Best drunk in August 2025." I would like to thank the beer company for this prestigious award.

—

I love algebra, trigonometry, and calculus. But geometry is where I draw the line.

—

Cars today have far too many confusing gadgets. For example, I tried to reverse, and all the car did was play a video of someone getting run over by a car from the car's point of view.

—

This one time I spent an entire month building a model of Mount Everest. People asked me if it was to scale. I told them no, it was to look at.

—

The other day a stranger I met asked if he could have my name. I told him, "No, I'm using it. Get your own."

What do you call a fish with no eyes. A fsh!

—

I've been trying to break up with an optician, but every time I say I can't see her anymore she moves an inch closer and says, "How about now?"

—

My mother was so surprised when I told her I was born again. She said she didn't feel a thing!

—

Scientists have created a new cross between a watermelon and cauliflower. People who eat it get a sense of sadness known as meloncauli.

—

I recently turned to Google for help with a crossword puzzle. The clue was "dishonestly gaining an advantage" for eight letters. I felt bad for looking it up. It was cheating.

—

Someone asked me if I had plans for the Fall. It took me a moment to realize they meant "autumn" not the collapse of civilization.

—

If, like me, you've ever been accused of being raised in a barn and walk to talk about it, remember, my door is always open.

You matter. Unless you multiply yourself by the speed of light. Then you energy.

—

I just read a book about Stockholm Syndrome. It was pretty bad at first, but by the end I really liked it.

—

A physicist and a biologist tried to have a relationship. But they had no chemistry.

—

When my wife turned 32, I told her we were only going to celebrate her birthday for half a minute. She was upset and asked why. I pointed out: "This is your thirty-second birthday."

—

The reason I believe aliens have never visited Earth is because our solar system has received terrible reviews. We only have one star.

—

I don't always time travel, but when I do, I did, and I will.

—

I asked a librarian if she had a book about Pavlov's dog and Schrodinger's cat. She said it rang a bell, but she wasn't sure if it was there or not.

There are eleven types of people in this world. Those who understand Roman numerals, and those who do not.

—

If I had a nickel for every time I didn't know what was going on...I would be like, "Why am I always getting all these nickels?"

—

I bought a dog from a blacksmith. As soon as I got it home it made a bolt for the door.

—

Defibrillators repulse me.

—

Purple is my favorite color. I love it more than red and blue combined.

—

A mummy covered in chocolate and nuts has been discovered in a tomb in Egypt. Archaeologists believe it may be Pharaoh Roche.

—

Some say that it's wrong to fill farm animals with helium, but I say "Whatever floats your goat!"

—

I just finished a training course to learn about the most effective way to create tunnels. It was boring.

I met my wife on Tinder. That was awkward.

—

A bus station is where a bus stops. A train station is where a train stops. It now make sense why I call my desk a work station.

—

If your nose goes on strike, pickett.

—

Everyone in our family is a musician. Even our sewing machine in a singer.

—

Dogs can bark over 500 times in a single day. That's just a ruff estimate.

—

It's been a tough day on Facebook. I still don't know what you're supposed to comment under a photo of a new baby. But I've learned it isn't "Yikes!"

—

The Pillsbury Dough Boy is a roll model.

—

I decided to rename my toilet Jim instead of John. People are really impressed when I tell them the first thing I do every morning is go to the Jim.

—

Those who jump off the Paris bridge are in Seine.

A truck loaded with thousands of copies of Roget's Thesaurus crashed yesterday losing its entire load. Witnesses were stunned, startled, aghast, taken aback, stupefied, confused, shocked, rattled, paralyzed, dazed, bewildered, mixed up, surprised, awed, dumbfounded, nonplussed, flabbergasted, astounded, amazed, confounded, astonished, overwhelmed, horrified, numbed, speechless, and perplexed.

—

I'd like to thank my middle finger for sticking up for me, particularly at those times I needed it the most.

—

When a microscope crashes into a telescope, they kaleidoscope.

—

I asked my surgeon if I could apply my own anesthesia. He said: "Go ahead. Knock yourself out."

—

A plateau is the highest form of flattery.

—

I'm starting a support group for people who talk too much. It'll be called: On and On Anon.

My friend recently lost three fingers in a work accident. He asked his doctor if he'd be able to drive using that hand. The doctor said, "Maybe, but I wouldn't count on it."

—

I'm writing a book about beer. I'm on my fifth draft today.

—

I tried one of those apps that show what you look like as an old person. It's called Camera.

—

I hope the weather this weekend is good for my trip to Puerto Backyardo. I'm getting tired of Los Livingroom.

—

I heard that the score in the game between the ocean and the beach was tide.

—

The worst pub I've ever been in was called The Fiddle. It was a vile inn.

—

Did you hear about the Italian chef that died? He pasta way. We cannoli do so much. His legacy will become a pizza history. He ran out of thyme.

—

You can't trust atoms. They make up everything!

I was the best man at my buddy's wedding in Paris. At the reception I raised my glass and said: "Eggs, cinnamon, bread, maple syrup." It was a French toast.

—

In Ancient Rome there were four types of poisons. Poisons I, II and III would kill you instantly. Poison IV would just make you extremely itchy.

—

My buddy just opened a restaurant called "Peace and Quiet" where the kids meals cost $300.

—

I was planning on buying Velcro™ shoes, but apparently, they're a rip-off.

—

I met a microbiologist the other day. They were quite a bit larger than I imagined they would be.

—

I was at the grocery store and the person bagging my groceries asked if I wanted paper or plastic. I said, "It doesn't matter. You choose."

He looked me straight in the eye and said, "No. YOU have to pick one."

Apparently, baggers can't be choosers.

I met a girl who sells batteries ideal for flashlights and toys down by the park. So basically, she sells C cells by the seesaw.

—

If Carpe Diem means seize the day, then maybe Crappy Diem means seizing the wrong day.

—

Shout out to the people who don't know what the opposite of in is.

—

I heard about these two slices of bread who went on a date. It was loaf at first sight.

—

My wife asked me to take her to one of those restaurants where they prepare the food right in front of her. So I brought her to Subway®.

—

The rotation of the earth makes my day.

—

After my funeral, my best friend is instructed to use my phone and send everyone a group text from my phone saying: "Thanks so much for coming."

—

Time flies like an arrow. Fruit flies like a banana.

You never see crabs volunteering to do any community service. I guess that's because they're shellfish.

—

My clothes are divided into three categories: Winter, Summer, and In Case I Lose Weight.

—

I was just at the gym and gave this new machine a real workout until I started to get sick. It's great though. It does everything. Snickers, KitKats, Mars bars, potato chips. The whole lot.

—

6:30 is the best time on the clock. Hands down.

—

I was a bookkeeper for many years. It didn't work out so well, because apparently the library wants them back.

—

Eye drops are technically blinker fluid.

—

Yesterday I called the paranoia hotline. The guy who answered said: "How the hell did you get this number?"

—

My wallet is like an onion. Every time I open it, I cry.

Siri kept calling me Shirley this morning and I was getting rather annoyed until I realized I'd left my phone in Airplane mode.

—

I decided to sell our vacuum cleaner. It was just gathering dust.

—

I heard that the more colorful your salad is the healthier it is for you. So I replaced the croutons with M&M's.

—

The inventor of the crossword puzzle moved into my neighborhood. He lives five streets across and two houses down.

—

I know a guy who just built an ATM that only gives out coins. I don't know why no one has thought of it before: it just makes cents!

—

I just saw three people jogging by the house. So it inspired me. To get up and shut the blinds.

—

My wife just yelled out at me: "You idiot! You haven't listened to a single word I've said, have you?" What a strange way to start a conversation.

Watch what you say around people who are allergic to egg whites. They can't take a yolk.

—

Instead of water, I put Redbull in my coffee maker this morning. I was halfway to work before I realized I forgot my car.

—

My barber said he can't cut my hair any longer. He can only cut it shorter.

—

I heard of a Roman Emperor who never aged after he turned 19. His name was Constant Teen.

—

I just paid $100 for a belt that doesn't even fit around me. What a huge waist!

—

Did I ever tell you about the time I went foraging for food in the forest and finally found a mushroom? It's a story with a morel at the end.

—

I can't believe my wife thinks I'm constantly invading her privacy. I just read about that in her diary.

—

Ewoks aren't meant to be left outside. They're Endor pets.

I went to the aquarium this weekend, but I didn't stay long. There was something fishy about that place.

—

I have a friend who wears sandals all year, no matter what the season. He's this French dude. His name is Philipe Fallop.

—

They held a neck decorating contest this week. I wanted to know who won. They told me it was a tie.

—

I know a produce manager who was unable to make it to work. He could drive, but he didn't avocado.

—

The other day I went to a silent auction. I won a dog whistle and two mimes.

—

A while back I threw a boomerang. Now I live in constant fear.

—

There was a break-in at the wig factory. Police are combing the area.

—

Did you hear about the shepherd who drove his sheep through town? He was given a ticket for making a ewe turn.

My buddy started a company selling trampolines disguised as prayer mats. Prophets are going through the roof!

—

The last job I was at paid me in vegetables. I left because I wasn't happy with my celery.

—

I put up flyers around the office to celebrate National Get It Wrong Week. But apparently it was last week.

—

My father loved crosswords puzzles so much he stipulated in his will that he should be buried six down and three across.

—

I planned to drive around all of the Great Lakes but only made it around four. I missed one. Which is Erie.

—

Nobody has heard a pterodactyl go to the bathroom because the P is silent.

—

I asked the librarian if she had any books on paranoia. She leaned forward and whispered: "They're right behind you!"

—

What's another word for Thesaurus? (Attribution: *Stephen Wright*)

I went to the doctor's because I was doing too many crosswords, and it was making me depressed. He told me not to get 2 down.

—

I tried donating blood the other day. Never again. Too many stupid questions. Whose blood is it? Where did you get it from? Why is it in a bucket?

—

You disliking classic gothic literature means you're my Edgar Allan Foe.

—

I shared a joke in a Zoom meeting yesterday, and nobody laughed. Turns out I'm not remotely funny.

—

I went shopping for a pair of camouflage pants the other day. But I couldn't find any.

—

Someone stole my mood ring the other day. I don't know how I feel about that.

—

My dog used to chase people on bikes. It got so bad that I had to finally take his bike away.

—

A friend of mine just got hired as the head of Old MacDonald's Farm.
   He's the new C-I-E-I-O.

My friend walked right into a big hole in the ground. I guess he just couldn't see that well.

—

A man just assaulted me with milk, cream, and butter. How dairy!

—

I told my wife she was drawing her eyebrows too high. She looked surprised.

—

I tried to write with a broken pencil, but it was pointless.

—

I was watching this frisbee and wondering why it was getting larger and larger. And then it hit me.

—

I just watched a documentary on how ships are put together. Riveting.

—

I was at a wedding this past weekend that was very emotional. Even the cake was in tiers.

—

I'm writing a book about all the things I should have done in my life. It's my Oughtabiography.

—

To the guy who invented zero. Thanks for nothing.

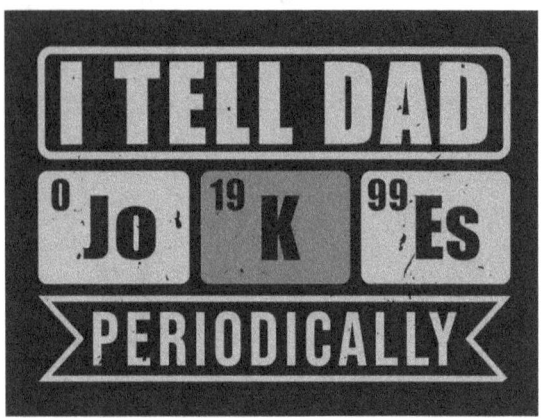

AMUSING REFLECTIONS

It's funny when you think about it.

Sometimes funny things are derived from re-exploring something you thought you knew. It might be visual; it might be conceptual. But the observations made are often amusing.

I thought it was the dryer that kept shrinking my clothes. Turns out it was the refrigerator all along.

—

I really miss the days when shouting out "Not it!" was an effective way of getting out of things you didn't want to do.

—

Effective Jan 20, 2025, *Air Force One* simultaneously became *Con Air*.

—

"Soup of the day" implies another, possibly even seductive, soup of the night.

—

I don't always carry all the groceries into my home on one arm, but when I do, my keys are in the wrong pocket.

—

The first 5 days after the weekend are the hardest.

—

I like to help people find things by pointing out that "it's got to be around here somewhere."

—

"Muffins" backwards is pretty much what you want to do when you take them out of the oven.

Caller ID isn't enough for me anymore. I want to know why someone is calling. I'd pay an extra $6.99 per month for "Caller Justification."

—

When someone emails you and then you email them back immediately, but they have an "out of office" autoreply, that's a digital equivalent of "Down Low! Too Slow!"

—

I wish I was a kid again so that everyone would be proud of me for taking a long nap.

—

I'd like to offer a shoutout to people who save their Word documents every two and a half seconds while working on them because they lost one file twenty-five years ago and refuse to have that ever happen to them again.

—

You are not stuck in traffic; you are traffic.

—

In limbo setting the bar very high means you're actually setting the bar really low. And vice versa.

—

Traditions are just dead people peer pressuring you.

If you start counting from zero, your lips won't press together until you reach one million.

—

If you ever think back to that era in film where movies with sound were called "talkies" and you think that's a little silly, consider the commonly accepted term "movie."

—

I used to think I was indecisive. But now I'm not so sure.

—

Even if a bear wears socks and shoes, he'll still have bear feet.

—

We should start referring to our age like levels in a video game instead of years. Because "I'm Level 56" sounds far better than just being an old person.

—

Cells multiply by dividing.

—

"Queue" is just "q" followed by 4 silent letters.

—

"Is pepsi" is "Is pepsi" backwards.

The time difference between 11 AM to 12 AM is 13 hours.

—

Isn't it interesting that the longer you don't pee, the longer you pee.

We squint at the sun because it's bright. But we usually squint at people because they're not.

—

Trees are stationary while alive and stationery when they're dead.

—

When you use a calculator, you become a calculator.

—

My question for paranoid people who check behind the shower curtain for murderers is: "What, exactly, is your plan if you find one?"

—

If you lose a thumb, you also lose your middle finger.

—

If the number 666 is considered evil. Then 25.8069758011 is the root of all evil.

—

People who take care of chickens are literally chicken tenders.

Those who don't study history are doomed to repeat it. But worse than that, those who do study history are doomed to watch helpless while those who didn't study it, repeat it.

—

When you think about it, it's the worst possible place for her to sell seashells.

—

Nothing refreshes my memory of what I need at the grocery store like that moment when I've just arrived home from the grocery store.

—

You're not scared of being alone in the dark. You're scared of not actually being alone in the dark.

—

Does anyone else find it disturbing that LEGO® people live in houses made from their own flesh?

—

The best liar you know is likely not the best liar you know.

—

Balloons are so weird when you think about it. "Happy Birthday! Here's a plastic sack of my breath."

As a kid I used to watch *The Wizard of Oz* and wonder how someone without a brain could talk. Then I got onto social media.

—

Potato chips are basically this: "Do you want to eat a potato one page at a time?"

—

I'm pretty certain that the person who put the first 'r' in February was also the person who decided how we should spell Wednesday.

—

Living with a dog is 90% following one another around, watching each other go potty, and wondering what the other has in their mouth.

—

I was assigned male at birth and identify as a man, but according to the back of the Kraft Dinner mac and cheese box I'm a family of four.

—

I remember being able to get up out of a chair without making sound effects. Good times!

—

Is the building called "the mall" because instead of going to one store you can go to "them all?"

You call them swear words. I call them sentence enhancers.

—

People will swim in the ocean even though there are many corpses in it. People will not swim in a pool with a single corpse in it. Humans have a corpse:water ratio that is acceptable for them to swim in.

—

Farts are the screams of trapped poop.

—

"Ohio" is just O saying hi to another O.

—

If you turn a floating canoe over, you can wear it as a hat. That's because it's cap sized.

—

Potatoes make French fries, chips, and vodka. It's like the other vegetables aren't even trying.

—

If you win a year's supply of calendars, you only win a single calendar.

—

The toaster was our pre-digital form of the pop-up notification.

—

I think he's old enough now to be able to change his name to Ryan Goose.

Just because you can connect to your neighbor's Bluetooth speaker and play ghost noises doesn't mean you should.

—

Most people don't realize that the opposite of a croissant is really just a happy uncle.

—

Eating too much cake is gluttony. But go ahead and eat as much pie as you want, because the sin of pie is always zero.

—

Life and beer are very similar. Chill for best results.

—

Some people are such treasures you just want to bury them.

—

Butterflies are not what they used to be.

—

I remember when my elementary school teachers used to say to us: "You won't have a calculator everywhere you go!" Well, we showed them!

—

Dijon vu: The same mustard as before.

—

What if there were no hypothetical questions?

You don't actually wash your hands. They wash each other while you stand there watching them like a creep.

—

If ignorance is bliss, there should be a lot more happy people.

—

If you watch JAWS backwards, it's a heartwarming story about a shark that gives arms and legs to disabled people.

—

Quick Animal Fact: Most bobcats are not actually named Bob.

—

Some people are wise. Some are otherwise.

—

When you buy a bigger bed, you have more bed room but less bedroom.

—

Did you realize that Bob The Builder and Jack The Ripper have the same middle name?

—

The only thing stopping pickles from being a breakfast food is you.

—

Even when your paper airplane flies, it's still stationery.

Grilled cheese is made by burning one side and then nervously undercooking the other.

—

To Err is Human. To Argh Is Pirate.

—

If a child refuses to sleep during nap time, are they guilty of resisting a rest?

—

Bacon cannot solve all your problems. That's what extra bacon is for.

—

Most people think that t-rexes can't clap because of their short arms, but it's mostly because they're extinct.

—

Whoever came up with the term "dentures" really missed the opportunity to coin them "substitooths."

—

Call me old fashioned, but I believe that a marriage should be between someone who can't stand pickles and a person who'd love to eat that extra pickle.

—

If you're feeling lonely, dim all the lights in your home and watch a few horror movies. Soon enough you'll no longer feel like you're alone.

Mayonnaise is basically sandwich lotion.

—

Snoring is basically bragging about being asleep so loudly that it stops other people from sleeping.

—

Minimalism is a scam created by Big Small to sell more less.

—

I just realized that the word "seven" has "even" in it. That's odd.

—

Laughing at your own mistakes can lengthen your life. But laughing at your wife's mistakes can shorten it.

—

Every pizza is a personal pizza if you believe in yourself.

—

I've been on Facebook now for almost 20 years. All this, at one time, used to be farmland.

—

If you are attracted to both men and women but neither are attracted to you that means you are Bi-yourself.

—

Atheism is a non-prophet organization.

Why do we say, "Slept like a baby?" Babies wake up every few hours crying. I want to sleep like a cat. A good 14 solid hours a day. No responsibilities. Zero life regrets.

—

When phones were connected to wires, people were free. Now that phones are wireless, people are tied to them.

—

If you can't look back at your younger self and realize that you were a bit of an idiot, you are probably still an idiot.

—

I just realized that "tater tots" is short for "potato toddlers" and I'm not sure how I feel about that.

—

You don't need a parachute to go skydiving. You need one to go skydiving more than once.

—

Fun facts: A burrito is just a rolled-up taco. A tostada? An unrolled taco. Nachos? Broken tacos. It's all just tacos.

—

Have you ever noticed that all instruments searching for intelligent life in the universe are pointed AWAY from Earth?

Bathroom hand dryers are amazing if you're looking for a way to kill a couple of minutes before wiping your still damp hands on your pants.

—

I love how Twix bars come with two in the package so you can eat one now and then save the other one for immediately after you finish the first one.

—

One spelling mistake can change your life. For example, when I was traveling for work, I texted my wife: "Having a great time here. I wish you were her."

—

I found this recipe that includes leftover bacon. It might as well require dragon loin or unicorn shanks.

—

My ducks may not be in a row, but at least they're having fun. Your ducks probably hate you for making them line up like that.

—

I suspect that after you die, your eyes are the last part of the human body to stop working That's because your pupils dilate.

—

Russian dolls are so full of themselves.

A baby's laughter is the most beautiful sound you'll ever hear. Unless it's 2:30 a.m., you're home alone, and you don't have a baby.

—

Any dog can be a guide dog if you don't care where you're going.

—

Knowledge is knowing Frankenstein isn't the monster.
Wisdom is knowing Frankenstein is the monster.

—

I'll bet when the knife was invented people thought it was the best thing since torn off chunks of bread.

—

Dr. Pepper is the name of the person who created it. What you're actually drinking is Dr. Pepper's monster.

—

The only thing worse than walking into a room with a box full of snakes, is walking into a room with a box that was SUPPOSED to be full of snakes.

—

Do you think he called himself T.S. Eliot so nobody would notice that T. Eliot is toilet spelled backwards?

If you don't pay your exorcist, do you get repossessed?

—

Have you ever noticed how many towns are named after water towers?

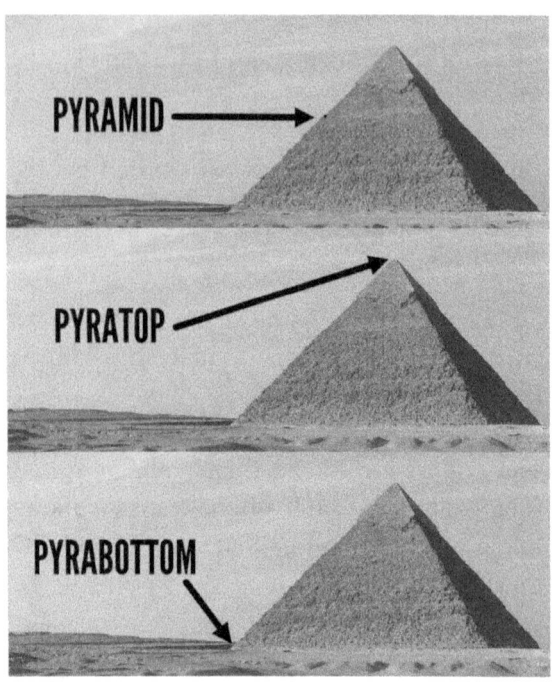

SHOWER THOUGHTS

Randon insightful or profoundly silly ideas
that come to mind when alone

*The strangest things come to mind often when
you're alone with your thoughts. And sometimes,
those thoughts can be quite amusing.*

I wonder if the person who coined the term "one hit wonder" ever came up with any other phrases.

—

I bet when cheetahs race and one of them cheats, one of them will yell out: "You're such a cheetah!" And then they all laugh, then go eat a zebra or whatever.

—

I don't know why you're not able to order a chocolate chip cookie medium rare.

—

The only problematic thing with eBooks is that, once I've finished reading them, I can't put them on my trophy shelf like a serial killer.

—

I often wonder what people have against the horse I rode in on.

—

Do clouds ever look down on us and say things like: "That one is shaped like an idiot?"

—

If it's really true that there are two sides to every story, then what do you say to the fact that no there aren't—there's only one?

If you weigh 99 pounds and you eat a pound of nachos, does that make you 1% nacho?

—

Is an elevator still an "elevator" when it is going down?

—

Have you ever noticed that the word bed is shaped like a type of bed?

—

I wonder if jellyfish are sad that there are no peanut butter fish.

—

What if the ocean is salty because the land never waves back at it?

—

If you wear a sweater and sweat, doesn't that make YOU the sweater?

—

When Beyonce and Jay-Z got engaged, did he ever refer to her as his Feyonce?

—

If a mother gives birth on the stairs, would that be considered her stepchild?

—

Why is it that tamales is pronounced tamales, but females is pronounced females instead of females?

If you use a teaspoon for measuring tea, what are tablespoons used for?

—

Why would you call it a butterfly when it should actually be called a flutterby?

—

Arms for your chairs are chairs for your arms.

—

If poison expires, does that make it more poisonous or less poisonous?

—

Your wife is also your ex-girlfriend.

—

Would a fly without wings be considered a walk?

—

To cannibals, most channels on television are food channels.

—

Would robots who fix one another be considered doctors or engineers?

—

If someone says, "don't listen to me," do you listen to them?

—

If the opposite of pro is con, then is the opposite of progress, congress?

If love is blind, why is there love at first sight?

—

If nothing is impossible then it is possible for something to be impossible.

—

The two e's in the word "bee" might actually be silent and we wouldn't really know.

—

Can you make a water bed bouncier if you use spring water?

—

Firetrucks are really water trucks.

—

What did bedbugs do before beds were invented?

—

Why is Monday so far from Friday, but Friday is so close to Monday?

—

Why is it that you can drink your drink but you can't food your food?

—

If James Bond is the world's most famous spy, wouldn't that make him the world's worst spy?

—

Why do we bake cookies and cook bacon?

If an octagon has 8 sides and an octopus has 8 legs, why is October not the 8th month?

—

Are leaves on trees called leaves because they leave the tree?

—

Whoever said "out of sight, out of mind" likely never had a spider disappear somewhere in the bedroom.

—

I can't even imagine the self-control required to work at a bubble wrap factory.

—

Egg salad is really chicken salad.

—

The first person who heard a parrot talk was probably not okay for several days.

—

I wonder how many vampires have been run over by people who back up using just their mirrors.

—

Did anyone ever get told the way to Sesame Street?

—

Why do eggs come in flimsy yet easy to open cartons and batteries come in a package you need a chainsaw to open?

Do memory foam mattresses sometimes wish they could forget?

—

I wonder if dogs understand what elevators are. Or when they get on one do they just think: "Okay, I'm getting into the world changer."?

—

Whatever happened to Old Zealand?

—

Do gun manuals have a trouble shooting section?

—

When two vegans get into an argument is it still called a beef?

—

Do people in Australia call the rest of the world "Up Over?"

—

Plagiarism is getting in trouble for something you didn't do.

—

Have we checked all food to see if exploding them makes them into something better or did we just stop with corn?

—

Why is it that people are never the right amount of whelmed?

A really smart TV would increase the volume when you started eating chips.

—

Do UK Websites use biscuits instead of cookies?

—

Sneezes are just basically face farts.

—

An apple a day will keep anyone away if you throw it hard enough.

—

Sometimes I think I'm reasonably intelligent, and sometimes I click the remote on my car door lock a second and third time for extra "lockiness."

—

Are people born with photographic memories, or does it take time to develop?

—

A belly button is basically a scar from a knife fight you got into with a person in a mask after being evicted from your first place.

—

I bet that if frogs wore shoes they'd be open-toad sandals.

—

Your stomach probably thinks that all potatoes are mashed.

I heard that Mars has no atmosphere. So, could we just create atmosphere by dimming the lights and playing smooth jazz?

—

How do nudists clear their glasses?

—

Why aren't iPhone chargers called Apple Juice?

—

If you're not supposed to drink WD40, why does it come with a little red straw?

—

There should be a calorie refund for things that don't taste as good as you'd expected.

—

If you're being chased by a pack of taxidermists, do not play dead.

—

Clapping your hands is just high-fiving yourself.

—

The object of golf is to play the least amount of golf.

—

If you sneeze and fart at the same time does your body take a screen shot?

PLEASE BEER WITH ME AS I SHARE SOMETHING THAT'S BARLY FUNNY

A SILLY JOKE WALKS INTO A BAR

Jokes about bars

"What is this, a joke?"

As a fan of craft beers, I walk into a lot of bars. It's fun, but not often funny, like these "walk(s) into a bar" jokes.

A rabbi, a priest, and a Lutheran minister walk into a bar. The bartender looks up and says, "Is this some kind of joke?"

—

A Roman walks into a bar holding up two fingers and says, "I'll have five beers please."

A priest, a Baptist, and a rabbit walk into a bar. The rabbit says: "I think I might be a typo."

—

A man walks into a bar. As he sits, he notices something hanging from the ceiling. A tenderloin, a ribeye, and a filet mignon.

He asks the bartender, "What's with the meat?

The bartender says, "If you can jump up and slap all three pieces at once, you get free drinks for an hour. If you miss even one, you have to pay for everyone else's drinks for the rest of the night. Wanna give it a go?"

The man takes another look at the meat, then says, "I think I'll pass. The steaks are too high."

—

A rabbi walks into a bar with a parrot on his shoulder. The bartender says, "Where did you get that?"

The parrot says, "Brooklyn, they're everywhere!" (Attribution: *Robin Williams*)

—

A neutron walks into a bar and asks how much it is for a beer.

"For you?" The bartender replies, "No charge."

A horse walks into a bar. The bartender says: "Hey!" The horse says: "Sure!"

—

A skeleton walks into a bar and orders a beer and a mop.

—

Three golf clubs walk into a bar. The putter asks for a beer. The wedge orders a salad and tequila. The third says: "Nothing for me, I'm the driver."

—

Sixteen sodium atoms walk into a bar followed by Batman.

—

Two conspiracy theorists walk into a bar. You can't tell me that it was just a coincidence.

—

A slice of pizza, a taco, and a hamburger walk into a bar. The bartender says: "I'm sorry, we don't serve food here."

—

Two buckets walk into a bar and the big one orders two beers. The bartender turns to the larger one who ordered and says: "Are you sure your friend really wants a drink? He looks a little pail."

Two dragons walk into a bar. The first one says: "It sure is hot in here." The bartender snaps back: "Shut your mouth!"

—

A man walks into a bar and sits down and orders a drink. The bartender says "I'm sorry sir, you already seem very drunk, I cannot serve you."

The guy gets up and leaves.

A few minutes later, the same man comes in again, sits down at the bar and tries ordering another drink.

I'm sorry sir, but I cannot serve you because you already seem drunk. Please leave.

The man gets up, grunts and wanders off again through the same exit.

Another few minutes go by, and the same guy comes back in, sits down and tries to order yet another drink.

"SIR," the bartender says in a firm voice. "I'VE ALREADY TOLD YOU TWICE NOW THAT YOU'RE TOO DRUNK AND I CANNOT SERVE YOU."

The man looks at the bartender all surprised and slurs: "How many bars do you work at?!!!"

Past, present, and future walk into a bar.
It was, is, and will be tense.

—

A bear walks into a bar and says ,"I'll have a gin and...tonic, please."

The bartender asks: "Why the long pause?"

The bear replies, "I don't know. I was just born with them."

—

A weasel walks into a bar. The bartender asks, "What can I get you?"

"Pop," goes the weasel.

—

A panda walks into a bar. It eats, shoots, and leaves.

—

A man walks into a bar and orders a drink. A minute later he hears: "You look great. Have you lost weight?" He looks around, but there's no one nearby.

A minute later, he hears: "You know, you don't look a day over 30."

He looks around again. There's no one but him and the bartender, so he asks "Did you hear that?"

The bartender points at a bowl of nuts on the bar top. "It's the peanuts. They're complimentary."

A horse walks into a bar. The bartender says: "Why the long face?"

—

A snake walks into a bar. The bartender says, "How the hell did you do that?"

—

Two guys walk into a bar. The third one ducks.

—

A dung beetle walks into a bar and asks, "Is this stool taken?"

—

A grizzled old sea captain walks into a bar. He has a peg leg, an eye patch, and a hook hand. The captain sits down and orders a drink.

The bartender serves it and asks the captain a question. "If you don't mind, how did you get that peg leg"

"I were chasing the white whale, laddy! Dangerous business!"

"Well, how did you get the hook hand?"

"Yar, had me a swashbuckling accident!"

"Wow! Well, what about the eye patch?"

"A seagull pooped in me eye."

"What?" Asks the bartender. "How did you lose your eye from seagull poop?"

"Yar, t'were me first day with the hook."

A blind man walks into a bar. Then a table. Then a chair.

—

A guy walks into a bar and asks for 10 shots of their finest single malt scotch. The bartender sets him up, and the guy takes the first shot in the row and pours it onto the floor. He then takes the last shot in the row and does the same. Finally, he starts drinking the remaining shots on the table.

"Excuse me," the bartender asks as he finishes off the eight shots. "Why did you do that?"

The guy replies, "Well the first shot always tastes like crap, and the last one always makes me sick!"

—

A tennis ball walks into a bar. The bartender says: "Have you been served?"

Three vampires walk into a bar.

The first one says, "I'll have a pint of blood."

The second one says, "I'll have one, too."

The third one says, "I'll have a pint of plasma."

The bartender says, "So, that'll be two Bloods and a Blood Lite?"

Julius Caesar walks into a bar and says, "I'll have a Martinus."

The bartender gives him a puzzled look and asks, "Don't you mean a Martini?"

"Look," Caesar replies, "If I wanted a double, I'd have asked for it!"

—

A mushroom walks into a bar and orders a drink, but the bartender yells at him to get out before he stinks up the place.

The mushroom looks taken aback and says, "Why? I'm a fun guy."

—

A three-legged dog walks into a saloon, his spurs clinking as he walks, his six-shooter slapping at his furry hip. He bellies up to the bar, stares down the bartender, and proclaims, "I'm looking for the man who shot my paw."

The NSA Walks into a bar.

"Hey, I've got a great new joke for you!" the bartender says.

The NSA smiles. "Heard it."

—

Comic Sans, Helvetica, and Times New Roman walk into a bar. "Get out!" the bartender shouts. "We don't serve your type here."

This cowboy walks into a bar. His hat is made of brown wrapping paper, his shirt and vest are made of waxed paper, and his chaps, pants, and boots are made of tissue paper. Pretty soon they arrest him for rustling.

—

A con man, a convicted felon, a grifter, and a pedophile walk into a bar. The bartender says, "You're here by yourself today, Donald?"

—

A ghost walks into a bar and orders a whiskey. The bartender says: "Sorry, we don't serve spirits here."

—

A bartender says, "We don't serve time travelers in here."

A time traveler walks into a bar.

—

A mobius strip walks into a bar and says, "Give me a drink, please, I've had quite the day."

The bartender says, "What's wrong?"

The mobius strip replies: "I don't even know where to begin."

—

A guy walks into a bar. He sucks at limbo.

An Irishman walks into a bar in New York City and orders three pints of beer. He drinks each one in turn and walks out.

The next night he returns, and again orders three pints of beer, and then again the next night. The bartender offers to serve them consecutively, so they won't go flat.

The Irishman explains, "I'd rather see them all lined up before me. I left two brothers behind in Ireland, and since we used to meet at the pub every night and have a pint together, I feel closer to them when I come drink my pint and their two."

This goes on for a year, and then one night, the Irishman fails to come in. The regulars are concerned and then saddened when he returns a few nights later and orders only two pints of beer.

When the bartender serves him, he says, "I see you didn't order a beer for one of your brothers. My condolences on your loss."

"My brothers are still alive," the Irishman says. "I didn't order my own beer; my wife made me promise to give up drinking."

—

An amnesiac walks into a bar. He approaches a beautiful blonde woman and says: "So, do I come here often?"

A five-dollar bill walks into a bar. The bartender says: "Hey, this is a singles bar!"

—

A guy walks into a bar and orders 30 shots of their most expensive whiskey.

As the bartender is setting up the shots the man starts knocking them back like crazy. He keeps at it until he drinks every single one.

The bartender says, "I have NEVER seen someone drink like that!"

The guy says, "If you had what I had you'd drink like that too."

"What do you have?"

"About 50 cents."

—

A screwdriver walks into a bar. The bartender says: "Hey! We have a drink named after you!"

The screwdriver says: "You have a drink named Philip?"

—

Jesus and his disciples walk into a bar. "Two waters, please," Jesus says, then winks.

—

A guy walks into a bar and asks for a fruit punch. The bartender says: "Sure, just get in that line." The guy looks around and gets confused, because there's no punch line.

Jimmy   Wales*   walks   into   a   bar.
[citation needed]
* Jimmy Wales is the founder of Wikipedia

—

A man walks into a bar with a chunk of asphalt under his arm. He asks for two beers. One for himself. And one for the road.

—

Two jumper cables walk into a bar. One of them says: "We'd like a couple of beers, please."
   The bartender says: "Okay, but don't you two start anything."

—

f(x) walks into a bar. The bartender says: "Sorry, we don't cater for functions."

—

A man walks into a bar owned and run by horses. The bartender says: "Why the short face?"

—

A corn stalk walks into a bar. The bartender says: "Want to hear a joke?"
   The corn stalk says: "I'm all ears!"

—

C, Eb, and G walk into a bar. The bartender, upon seeing them, says, "Sorry, we don't serve minors.

Helium, Neon, and Argon walk into a bar. The bartender says: "Sorry, we don't serve noble gas here." None of the three of them react.

—

An Englishman, an Irishman, a Scotsman, a Welshman, a Frenchman, a German, an Italian, a Swede, two Finns, a Norwegian, a Dane, a Greenlander, an Austrian, a Hungarian, a Pole, a Lithuanian, a Latvian, an Estonian, a Russian, a Turk, an Egyptian, a Palestinian, an Israeli, a Greek, a Macedonian, a Moldovan, a Chinese guy, a Japanese guy, a Laotian, a Vietnamese guy, a Cambodian, a North Korean, a South Korean, an American, a Mexican, a Canadian, a Brazilian, an Australian, a New Zealander, a South African, a Libyan, a Moroccan, a Spaniard and a Cuban try to walk into a fancy cocktail bar.

The bouncer says, "Sorry, lads...you can't come in without a Thai."

—

A grasshopper walks into a bar. "Did you know," the bartender asks, "that there's a drink named after you?"

The grasshopper says: "You have a drink named Bob?"

A new lawyer walks into a diner. "Where's the bar?" he asks the waiter.

The waiter responds, "You passed it on the way here."

—

A beaver walks into a bar. The bartender yells "Close the dam door!"

—

Three intransitive verbs walk into a bar. They sit. They drink. They leave.

—

A pun, a play on words, and a limerick walk into a bar. No joke.

A man walks into a bar and asks for a beer. The bartender says: "Sure, if you can name two pronouns."

"Who? Me?" the man says?

"Here's your beer," the bartender replies.

—

A man with authority walks into a bar. He orders everyone around.

—

Give a man a duck and he'll eat for a day. Teach a man to duck and he'll never walk into a bar.

—

A termite walks into a bar and asks: "Hey, is your bar tender here?"

A Shetland pony walks into a bar. The bartender asks what he'll have.

"I'll have a whisky," the pony whispers.

"Okay," says the bartender. "But why are you whispering?"

"I'm a little horse."

—

A snail walks into a bar and orders a drink. The bartender says, "We don't serve your kind here!" and throws him out.

Two weeks later the same snail comes back and says to the bartender. "What the hell was that for?"

—

A diamond walks into a bar full of his coal friends and says. "I know, I know. Look, I've been under a lot of pressure."

—

A man walks into a bar and orders a whiskey, neat. When the bartender serves it in a glass he just finished cleaning, the man pulls out a straw and drinks from it.

"I'm terribly sorry, is the glass dirty?" the bartender asks.

"No," the man says. "I just promised my wife I'd never put my lips on another glass of whiskey again."

A man walks into a bar with an apple pie balanced on the top of his head.

The bartender asks: "Why are you wearing an apple pie on your head?"

The man replies: "Because it's a Tuesday. And my family has a tradition. We always wear apply pies on our heads on Tuesdays." The bartender says: "But it's Wednesday."

Sheepishly, the man says: "Oh gee, I must look like a real fool."

—

An Irishman walks into a bar in at Toronto airport and orders a drink. He drinks it quickly. Then he orders another one. He drinks it down right away.

When he orders his third within his first three minutes, the bartender figures he'll engage in some conversation to slow him down a little. "Is that an Irish accent I detect?" he asks.

"It sure is," the patron replies.

"What brings you to Canada?"

The Irishman says, "Well, I was in a pub in Dublin and the coaster under my glass read 'Drink Canada Dry' so I thought I'd come over and give it a shot."

An Apple walks into a bar, orders the same drink as yesterday, but pays more.

—

A Redditor walks into a bar. v
Sorry, I think my CTRL key is broken.

—

A horse walks into a bar. The bartender asks, "Hey, why the long face? Are you depressed?"

The horse ponders for a second, scratches his chin, and says, "I don't think I am" and promptly disappears.

You see, this is a joke about Rene Descartes' famous statement "I think, therefore I am" and I could have mentioned this at the start of the joke, but that would be putting Descartes before the horse.

Before the invention of the crowbar, crows had to drink at home.

HALLOWEEN

It's the best month of the year.

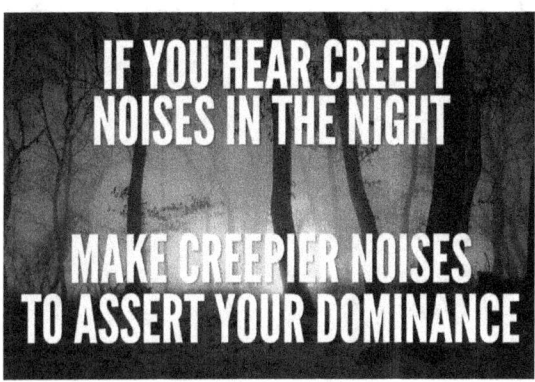

These are dad jokes, moan-inducing puns, and silliness related to the spooky, the eerie and the most wonderful time of the year.

I threw a boomerang at a ghost the other day. I knew it would come back to haunt me.

—

To kill a French vampire, you need to drive a baguette through its heart. Sounds easy, but the process is painstaking.

Goth corn is also known as corn on the macabre.

—

Whoever determined that a 1-inch candy bar is "fun-sized" should really evaluate their standard for entertainment.

—

Dyslexic zombies only eat Brians.

—

Me: "There's only one thing that scares me at Halloween."
My Wife: "Which is?"
Me: "Exactly!"

—

I bought 80% shares in a vampire hunting company. That's right, I'm the main stakeholder.

—

My neighborhood pub has a special Halloween hot dog and a beer combo. They call it the Frank & Stein Special.

—

My wife and I dressed up as a pair of sexy screwdrivers for Halloween. Boy, did we ever turn a lot of heads!

—

When you teach a wolf to meditate, he becomes aware wolf.

When a man doesn't realize he's a lycanthrope, he's an unaware wolf.

—

Ghosts like to ride in elevators because it lifts their spirits.

—

I saw a snowman with a six pack. I think he was the abdominal snowman.

—

Ghosts don't go trick-or-treating because they have no body to go with.

—

Guess who has 7 thumbs and just got fired from the morgue?

—

At his death bed, Achilles realized that they were going to lose the war and uttered his last words, "Defeet hurts."

—

Will glass coffins be a success? Remains to be seen.

—

Trick-or-treating with twin witches can be confusing because you never know which witch is which.

—

Being cremated is my last hope for a smokin' hot body.

The Man Who Created Autocorrect Has Died. Restaurant In Peace.

—

How do you know a person is a werewolf and not just someone with a beast infection?

—

A cartoonist was found dead in his home. The details are sketchy.

—

The skeleton knew it was going to rain on Halloween because he felt it in his bones.

—

Being a funeral director is a dying profession.

—

When the pirate's obese parrot died, it was a real weight off of his shoulder.

—

Nobody wants to go Trick-or-Treating with Dracula because he's a pain in the neck.

—

I thought about opening up a funeral home, but it seems like it would be a large *undertaking*.

—

My favorite literary vampire is the one from Sesame Street. Some people tell me that he doesn't count, but I know that he most definitely does.

Did you hear about the werewolf who was invited to the dance? He wanted to go, but the full moon was giving him paws.

—

The scarecrow comedian got booed because all of his jokes were too corny.

—

My house was bitten by a werewolf. Now, in the light of a full moon, it becomes a werehouse. Not evil or anything, just more storage space.

—

Ghosts are terrible liars because you can see right through them.

—

Mummies rarely take vacations because they're afraid to unwind.

—

Cemeteries are the best place to write because they have so many plots.

—

Skeletons don't go to scary movies because they don't have the guts.

—

When you die people cry and beg for you to come back. But when you do, there's always running and screaming.

Every year the Boogie Man always wins the Halloween dance contest.

—

Demons and ghouls like to hang out together because a demon is a ghoul's best friend.

—

If pumpkins wrote books, they would likely be considered pulp fiction.

—

I'm not afraid of a werewolf; I'm afraid of a righttherewolf.

—

The opposite of formaldehyde is casualdejekyll.

—

Did you hear about the scarecrow who won the Nobel Peace Prize? He was outstanding in his field.

—

Spiders and snakes are a vital part of the eeks-osystem.

—

Our house is haunted by a chicken. A poultrygeist. It's a fowl spirit. We need an eggsorcist to help it cross to the other side.

MUSIC

Dad jokes, puns, and humor from the world of music.

Silly puns about songs, songwriters and performers are music to my ears.

The song "We're Not Gonna Take It" came out four decades ago, but it feels like we have, in fact, continued to take it.

—

I stopped believing for a little while this morning. Journey is going to be so disappointed in me if they ever find out.

—

If Celine Dion's name was only the vowels, it'd be a line of lyrics from Old MacDonald Had a Farm.

—

There's nothing worse than having a Cranberries song stuck in your head, in your head, in your heeeaaaad...

—

Two wind turbines were sitting on a hill. One asks the other, "Do you have a favorite song?"

The other replies, "Well...all my life I have been a heavy metal fan."

—

I've named my printer Bob Marley because it keeps on jammin.'

—

"Meatloaf" is one of the best safe words you can use, because it means "I would do anything for love, but I won't do that."

Last night I had a dream that disco was making a comeback. At first, I was afraid, I was petrified.

—

A strange virus has spread causing people to forget all about 80s rock bands. Nobody knows The Cure.

—

Larva was a great band before The Beatles emerged.

—

I was in a band called The Hinges. We opened for The Doors.

—

I kind of wished Dolly sang 10-2 instead. That's my kind of way to make a living.

—

Retired basketball great Shaquille O'Neal can't end his letters or messages with "Love, Shaq." The B-52s ruined that for him.

—

I just bought a sweet car online. It used to be owned by Neil Diamond.

—

The Beastie Boys must be so disappointed in me when I stay home by myself and go to bed at 9 PM after they fought so hard for my rights.

Michael Jackson put out some amazing albums in his lifetime. But I'm sure we can all agree that his 7th album was Bad.

—

Do people in electric cars listen to AC/DC... or something more current?

—

Nobody wants to listen to Whitesnake with me. So here I go again on my own.

—

People said I'd never get over my obsession with 80s Phil Collins hits. But take a look at me now.

—

Someone asked me for my opinion about The Rolling Stones, but don't even get me started. Because if you start me up, I'll never stop.

—

In a parallel universe, Mariah Carey is doing her holiday shopping and is sick of hearing me on every store's speaker system.

—

The best way to learn how heavy a chili pepper is...is to give it a weigh, give it a weigh, give it weigh now.

—

My buddy is in a rock cover band. They're called Paper.

I don't always whoop, but when I do, there it is.

—

When my wife asked if I could stop playing "Wonderwall" by Oasis on repeat I said "Maybe..."

—

That moment when you realized who sang the song "Take On Me."

—

If the singer from Foo Fighters shaved, he'd look just like the drummer from Nirvana.

—

I lost my pizza cutter, so I used a Bryan Adams CD. It cuts like a knife.

—

What if Jessie's Girl was Stacey's Mom and her number was 8675309?

—

The sad news is that I needed to break up with my girlfriend Lorraine because I wanted to start going with another girl named Claralee. But the good news is that I can see Claralee now, Lorraine is gone.

—

Avril Lavigne could have just called her song Skater Boy instead of Sk8er Boi. Why'd she have to go and make things so complicated?

I bought some lettuce yesterday from a grocery store called Mamas and Papas. But I can't eat it because all the leaves are brown.

—

I wrote a song about a tortilla once. It's more like a wrap.

—

I tried to cut the grass yesterday, but it didn't go so well. I fought the lawn and the lawn won.

—

The other night I played a U2-themed game called Bonopoly. It's like regular Monopoly, but where the streets have no name.

—

Whenever I hear a Milli Vanilli song I don't sing it. I just move my lips. They would have wanted it that way.

—

The difference between Black Eyed Peas and chickpeas is that Black Eyed Peas can sing us a song and chickpeas can only hummus one.

—

Mariah Carey opening the song with "I don't want a lot for Christmas" and then revealing all she wants is "you" is such a good burn.

—

My laptop keeps singing "Hello." It's a Dell.

My friend Joe recently went on the Dolly Parton diet. It really made Joe lean, Joe lean, Joe lean, Joe lean.

—

Whitney Houston's favorite type of coordination was "Hand Eyeeeee!"

—

Whenever someone yells "Stop!" I don't know if it's in the name of love, it's hammer time, or if I should collaborate and listen.

—

I used to be addicted to quoting Taylor Swift songs, but I think I am finally clean.

—

Cassette tapes had a side A and a side B. So it's only logical that their successor would be CD.

—

ABBA are the only palindromic act to have a palindromic hit (SOS) in a palindromic genre (POP).

—

If 5-4 is Star Wars Day, can 9-25 be Dolly Parton Day?

—

I have a friend who writes songs about sewing machines. He's a Singer songwriter, or sew it seams.

Sweet dreams are made of cheese. Who am I to dis a brie. I cheddar the world for feta cheese. Everybody needs a Stilton.

—

"Ask not what your saxophone can do for you; ask what you can do for your saxophone." - John F. Kenny G.

—

My friend can make a made-to-measure suit in an hour. I call him Taylor Swift.

—

After playing guitar for years, I thought I could learn to play the piano. But it's not an easy instrument to pick up.

—

I recently saw a radio for sale. The ad said it was being sold for $1 because it was stuck on full volume. I thought, "I can't turn that down."

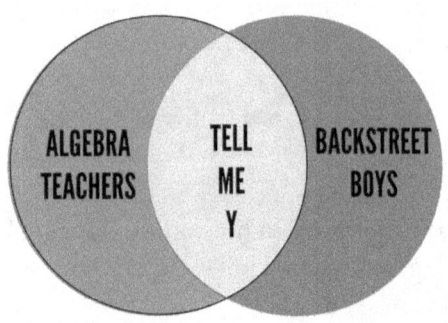

I THINK IT'S A SIGN

Sign funnies.

Many of the jokes I've shared on the sign outside our house read like headlines or other notices. And some just work better as visual content.

I have a couple of sock puppets for sale. Is anyone willing to take them off my hands?

—

Breaking News: A woman at the airport fainted and fell onto the baggage carousel. But she's slowly coming around now.

—

Autopsy Club meeting next Wednesday. Open Mike Night.

—

Feeling a bit paranoid? Remember…you're not alone.

WANTED: Someone to hand-feed me Doritos while I knit baseball caps for squirrels, so my fingers don't get orange. No weirdos.

—

Man in underwear leads police in brief chase.

—

I can't remember how to write 1, 1000, 51, 6, and 500 in Roman Numerals.
   I M LI VI D.

—

Relish today. Ketchup tomorrow.

—

If you're here for the yodeling lesson please form an orderly, orderly, orderly queue.

—

Overeaters Anonymous Hotline:
888-888-8888

—

"Dear Diet Coke. I feel like you are over-reacting." —Sincerely, Mentos

—

Texting and driving is not wreckommended.

—

National Apathy Society. Become a member. Or not. We don't care.

—

Broken barometer for sale. No pressure.

To the thief who stole my glasses. I will find you. I have contacts.

—

If you hate speeding tickets, raise your right foot.

—

Broken drum for sale. Great price. You just can't beat it.

—

The 3 symptoms of laziness:
  #1

—

If you believe in telekinesis, raise my hand.

—

A seminar on time travel will be held here last month.

—

Boycott shampoo. Demand the real poo.

—

Lif is too short.

—

In search of fresh vegetable puns. Lettuce know.

—

Afraid of Santa? You may be claustrophobic.

—

I before E except after C was disproved by SCIENCE.

This is how the moon would look if it was colonized: M:O:O:N

—

Choose cremation. You urned it.

—

If you play guitar and want to know the secret to making it sound better, please stay tuned.

—

Sting has been kidnapped. The Police have no lead.

—

Spring is here. I got so excited I wet my plants!

—

The first rule of Introvert Club:
1. There is no Introvert Club
   Whew! Thank goodness.

—

Wanted: Someone to brush their teeth with me because 4 out of 5 dentists say brushing alone won't help prevent tooth decay. No weirdos please.

—

If you get a DM from me about canned meat, don't open it. It's spam.

—

Geology rocks but Geography is where it's at!

I'm giving up drinking for a month. Sorry, that came out wrong. I'm giving up. Drinking for a month.

—

My wife won't karaoke with me. I have to duet alone.

—

The Institute of Unfinished Research has concluded that 6 out of 10 people

"Our specialty is the Synonym Roll."

LANGUAGE

*Musings that play upon oddities about
language, grammar, and more.*

**YOU CAN'T RUN THROUGH A CAMPSITE.
YOU CAN ONLY RAN, SINCE IT'S PAST TENTS.**

*I regularly nerd out on jokes related to language
play and use. And the English language is definitely an odd one.*

The difference between a kleptomaniac and
a literalist is a comma. The literalist takes
things literally. The kleptomaniac takes
things, literally.

—

Why do we pronounce the g in longevity
twice?

The fact that some people can't distinguish between etymology and entomology bugs me in ways I can't put into words.

—

What is a four-letter word with a little laugh in the middle. It really is.

—

Hyphenated.
Non-hyphenated.
The irony.

—

Is spelt spelled spelt or spelled?

—

If the sentence "give her her book" is correct, then why is "give him him book" wrong?

—

Sadly, the days of people using proper English are went.

—

If you replace the "W" with a "T" in When, Where, and What, you get the answer for each question.

—

What word can you make shorter when you add two letters to it? Short.

—

Dark is spelled with a k because you can't c in the dark.

If you can't tie a knot, you can not. If you can, you can knot.

—

I hate spelling errors. If you mix up just a couple of letters your whole sentence is urined.

—

What has 4 letters, sometimes 9 letters, but never has 5 letters.

—

Before was was was was was is.

—

Incorrectly is the only word that, when spelled incorrectly is spelled correctly.

—

Pre- means before. *Post-* means after. Using both at the same time would be preposterous.

—

I think I prefer the British spelling of "diarrhea" which is "diarrhoea" because it really looks like you lost control of your vowels.

—

In England "booster shot" is spelled borchestershire shot"

—

Can February March? No but April May.

Minute and minute shouldn't be spelled the same. I'm not content with this content. I object to that object. I need to read what I read again. Excuse me but there's no excuse for this. Someone should wind this post up and throw it in the wind.

—

My favorite things are eating my pets and not using commas.

—

What has four letters often has five letters and always ends with an S. That's a statement. And I think it's missing some commas.

—

If you identify a UFO as a UFO then it becomes an FO. Unless it has landed. Then, it's simply an O.

—

My father has the heart of a lion, and a lifetime ban from the zoo.

—

Whoever put the letter b in the word subtle deserves a pat on the back.

—

A hyperbole is, without a doubt, the single most magnificent thing that has ever happened in the world ever.

ADULT

Jokes that include adult language or situations. Parental discretion is advised.

These are the types of jokes I'd never put on the chalk board in front of the house, because we try to keep it family friendly, but I did still collect them, and I get to share them here.

Is "buttcheeks" one word, or should I spread them apart?

—

When a chameleon can't change its colors anymore that might be a sign of a reptile dysfunction.

You know what really burns my ass? Flames about three feet high.

—

The more hair I lose the more head I get.

—

I went to a zoo the other day and the only animal in the entire place was a dog. It was a Shih Tzu.

—

It turns out a creampie isn't a pastry and the internet is a truly disgusting place.

—

Life is like toilet paper. You're either on a roll or taking shit from some asshole.

—

Never fight with a dinosaur. You're likely to get Jurasskicked.

—

Those who confuse burro and burrow don't know their ass from a hole in the ground.

—

Avoid dangerous cults. Practice safe sects.

—

There's no place like home, where the ho and me come together.

—

Pollen: When flowers just can't keep it in their plants.

Maybe the Grinch would be nicer if every five minutes some dude wasn't singing about what a piece of shit he is.

—

A dog is able to learn as many as 250 words and gestures, can count to 5 and perform simple math. Equivalent human age: 3. A cat doesn't give a f*ck and is sick of your shit. Equivalent human age: 43.

—

My wife told me that sex is better on holiday. That wasn't a very pleasant postcard to receive.

—

I once thought that alcoholics ran in my family. But that's not true. They mostly stumble around and break shit.

—

I've heard of this great new fragrance for introverts. It's called "Leave Me The Fug" cologne.

—

69% of people find something dirty in everything they read.

—

According to HR, calling a co-worker foreskin because they disappear when things get hard is not appropriate.

A blue whale's anus can stretch to approximately 3 and a half feet, making it the second largest asshole on the planet—just behind people who talk on speakerphone in public.

—

I hate when I lose things at work. Like my favorite pen, or my f*cking will to live.

—

I've learned that I'm f*cktose intolerant. It's the condition of being completely unable to tolerate other people's bullshit.

—

How would you cancel an appointment at a sperm bank. Do you just call them up and announce that you can't come?

—

"I'm sorry" and "I apologize" usually mean the same thing...but not at a funeral. English is a weird language.

—

I thought my vasectomy would keep my wife from getting pregnant, but apparently it only changes the color of the baby.

—

Coffee spelled backwards is eeffoc. Just know that I don't really give eeffoc until I've had my coffee.

"Is there a name that we call people who waste our time? If not, I suggest clocksucker." —(Attribution: *Snarky Nana*)

—

My friend told me he performed as a ventriloquist to put himself through med school to become a proctologist. I think he is talking out of his ass.

—

I was flirting with a woman at a party and asked if she was into role play. She said, "Yeah, I like to dress up as 25 letters of the alphabet." She saw my confused look, leaned in and said "Because I'm not E."

—

I'm opening a bar that hosts brass bands every night. It's called HornHub.

—

What has two butts and kills people? An assassin.

—

Carving a pumpkin in September is called premature ejackolantern.

—

The fact that "hemorrhoids" aren't called "asteroids" is a major missed opportunity for science, health, and the English language.

Male bees die after mating. That's basically their life: Honey. Nut. Cheerio.

—

What did the left leg say to the right leg? "That guy in the middle is a bit of a dick, isn't he?"

—

Two cannibals are eating a clown. The one looks at the other and asks, "Does this taste funny to you?"

—

Scientists have created a laughing gas that's also a laxative. They did it for shits and giggles.

—

Miss Piggy can't count to ten because at 69 she gets a frog in her throat.

—

How may flies does it take to screw in a lightbulb?
   Two. But the real question is: "How did they get in there?"

—

Without nipples, boobs would be pointless.

—

Sign on an out-of-business brothel: Beat it. We're closed!

Porn gives young people an unrealistic and unhealthy idea of how quickly a plumber will come to your house.

—

There isn't a pregnant Barbie doll because Ken came in another box.

—

A buddy of mine who recently converted to Judaism opted for the cheapest circumcision he could find. He said it was a real rip-off.

—

Did you hear about the guy who got a Viagra pill stuck in his throat? He's suffering from a stiff neck now.

—

The Titanic is a great example of how just "the tip" can get you in a lot of trouble.

—

Horrible pick-up line: Is that a mirror in your pocket? Because I can see myself in your pants.

—

The difference between a golf ball and a G-spot is that most men will actually search for a golf ball.

—

A nanny with breast implants might be called a faux-pair.

Apparently someone in London gets stabbed every 52 seconds. Poor bastard!

—

If you're riding a horse full speed and there's a giraffe next to you and a lion is chasing you the best thing you should do is to get your drunk ass off the carousel.

—

What gets longer when pulled, works best when jerked, and inserts into a slot?

A seatbelt.

—

I am now at the age where picking up a hottie at the club usually means buying a rotisserie chicken at Costco.

—

I accidentally swallowed a bag of Scrabble tiles. My next trip to the bathroom could spell disaster.

—

I was at the bar the other night when a waitress screamed out: "Does anyone know CPR?"

"I do," I called out. "Hell, I know the whole alphabet."

Everyone laughed.

Well, except for this one guy.

Well, you have reached the end of this book, my friend. I sincerely hope that it brought you at least a few laughs and/or smiles.

If you enjoyed this book, I would greatly appreciate an honest review wherever you acquired it. Or better yet, use one of these collected jokes to spread a smile or laugh to someone else. The world could definitely use more of that.

Mark Leslie

ACKNOWLEDGEMENTS

I would like to acknowledge all the folks in the Lexington/University Downs and adjacent neighborhoods who have supported my "daily dad jokes" over the years, especially Dana, Christine, and Andrew, for allowing me to share a few jokes in honor of the latter two's September 2025 nuptials.

Seriously, Liz and I have the absolute best neighbors. We're lucky to be surrounded on all sides by amazing people we admire and adore.

Speaking of Liz, I want to thank her for putting up with my goofy jokes and also enabling my silliness with such finely crafted woodworking skills.

Thanks also to the numerous friends around the world who regularly share fun jokes, visual humor, and other silliness with me, especially Kathy Rapsky and Jack Spink.

Unless otherwise stated below, all images used in this book are the property of the author. Image licenses have been purchased/acquired via the following sources and were either used as acquired or with additions/edits/modifications as noted.

IMAGE ATTRIBUTION

Page 6 - "Dad Joke Loading Please Wait" - Sodha Manalika/stock.adobe.com

Page 21 - "Dad Jokes/Rad Jokes" - creativeproartist/stock.adobe.com

Page 29 - "Bad puns are how eye roll" - Adobe (db/stock.adobe.com)

Page 98 - "Swear Jar/Bad Puns Jar" - (Generated Asset/stock.adobe.com) with customized content

Page 98 - "Funny dad jokes shirt design periodic table elements" (Tee Vibe Design/stock.adobe.com)

Page 99 - "Observation Deck" - Image: CS604425 CartoonStock.com

Page 114 - "The Great pyramid of Giza" (Omar Baghdady/stock.adobe.com) with customized content

Page 115 - "Cartoon shower with thought bubble" (lineartestpilot/adobe.stock.com) added to personal photo

Page 125 - "What is this, a joke?" - created with the assistance of OpenAI's ChatGPT (GPT-5) / DALL·E

Page 141 - "Crow Bar" - created with the assistance of OpenAI's ChatGPT (GPT-5) / DALL·E

Page 142 - "Vampire Pick-Up Lines" - created with the assistance of OpenAI's ChatGPT (GPT-5) / DALL·E

Page 143 - "Dark misty forest" (Melinda Nagy/stock.adobe.com) with customized content

Page 149 - "A-Ha: 1985. LP front cover" Rajko Simunovic Alamy ID: 2ED8176 with customized content

Page 157 - "Small tropical island" (Panya/stock.adobe.com) with customized content

Page 161 - "Toronto Skyline" Adobe (rabbit75_fot/stock.adobe.com) with customized content

Page 162 - "Synonym Roll" - Image: CS603791 Cartoonstock.com

Page 163 - "You Can't Run Through a Campsite" - created with the assistance of OpenAI's ChatGPT (GPT-5) / DALL·E

Page 167 - "Backup Swear Jar And Swear Jar" (Laurent/stock.adobe.com)

YOU MIGHT ALSO LIKE

*The Canadian Mounted: A Trivia Guide
to Planes, Trains and Automobiles*

In the movie *Planes, Trains and Automobiles*,
John Candy is seen holding a paperback that,
in the original script written by John Hughes,
reads that Del Griffith is reading a porno-
graphic novel. It's a funny prop for the Canadian actor to be holding. This same book is
also seen in the *Deadpool* movies.

This re-imagined incarnation of *The Canadian Mounted* explores the use of this book
(both the real one and the later prop version
of it) and many other intriguing, insightful
and entertaining behind-the-scenes details as
they relate to the classic 1987 John Hughes
film.

Created for fans of the movie, this book
compiles stories related to the writing and
making of the film, curious tales and trivia
associated with it, including what inspired
Hughes to write the script, deleted scenes,
Ryan Reynolds' adoration of fellow Canadian actor John Candy, and more.

If you're a fan of *Planes, Trains and Automobiles* then this is a book you must read.

A TRIVIA GUIDE TO
PLANES, TRAINS
& AUTOMOBILES

THE
CANADIAN
MOUNTED

Yippee Ki-Yay Motherf*cker:
A Trivia Guide to Die Hard

When *Die Hard* premiered in July 1988, John McClane didn't just become a fly Hans Gruber's ointment, he ushered in a bold new era of action films, inspired countless knock-off action movies, and created a franchise that spanned five decades.

Even thirty-five years later this movie continues to inspire heated annual debates regarding the film's status as a Christmas movie.

This guide, lovingly researched by a die-hard (pun fully intended) fan collects trivia, behind-the-scenes stories of the movie, the script, the actors, and the books and other written material that *Die Hard* and several of the follow-up films in the franchise were based on or inspired by.

If you're a fan of *Die Hard,* then you're going to love this book.

MARK LESLIE

YIPPEE KI-YAY

MOTHER F*CKER!

A TRIVIA GUIDE
TO DIE HARD

Merry Christmas! Shitter was Full!
A Trivia Guide to National Lampoon's
Christmas Vacation

On December 1, 1989 the world was introduced to the third and most successful sequel in the *Vacation* franchise as Clark Griswold's dream of having a fun old-fashioned family Christmas descends into a hilarious nightmare of dark comedy misadventure.

Released on the 35th Anniversary of the film's premiere, this book is a celebration of the movie along with trivia and behind-the-scenes details related to *Christmas Vacation*, which originated from a John Hughes short story called "Christmas '59" originally published in the December 1980 issue of National Lampoon magazine.

If *National Lampoon's Christmas Vacation* is an annual must-watch film for you each holiday season, or it's a movie you enjoy quoting from "the whole year through" then you'll love this collection of fascinating details about the movie.

A TRIVIA GUIDE TO NATIONAL LAMPOON'S™
CHRISTMAS VACATION

MERRY CHRISTMAS!

SHITTER
WAS
FULL!

MARK LESLIE

ABOUT THE AUTHOR

Mark's first short story was published in 1992, the same year he started working as a bookseller in Ottawa, Ontario, Canada. He has since published more than forty books that include true ghost stories, urban fantasy, horror, and humor.

When he is not quoting lines from classic movies like *Christmas Vacation*, *Die Hard*, *Planes, Trains and Automobiles*, numerous Monty Python films and sketches, or television shows such as *Cheers*, *The Simpsons*, and *Perfect Strangers*, Mark can be found haunting local bookstores, libraries, and craft beer establishments.

You can find him and links to all his books online at www.markleslie.ca.

Author's note: *I wasn't sure what sort of author photo to use for this book. Author photos, like online profiles, can be a bit different depending on the environment.*

SELECTED BOOKS BY MARK LESLIE

Canadian Werewolf (Series)
A Canadian Werewolf in New York
Stowe Away
Fear and Longing in Los Angeles
Fright Nights, Big City
Lover's Moon (with Julie Strauss)
Hex and the City (with Julie Strauss)
Only Monsters in the Building
A Canadian Werewolf in London, Ontario

Non-Fiction Paranormal
Haunted Hamilton
Spooky Sudbury (with Jenny Jelen)
Tomes of Terror
Creepy Capital
Haunted Hospitals (with Rhonda Parrish)
Macabre Montreal (with Shanya Krishnasamy)

All books by Mark Leslie:
books2read.com/markleslie

www.ingramcontent.com/pod-product-compliance
Lightning Source LLC
Chambersburg PA
CBHW071742120626
46550CB00002B/625